FELICIA
CARTRIGHT
AND THE CASE OF THE
DANCING FIRE

Felicia

Joan

FELICIA CARTRIGHT

AND THE CASE OF THE DANCING FIRE

BERNARD PALMER

Cover Artwork: Adobe Firefly and Ideogram

Editor: Charlene Miskimen

Aneko Press *Youth*

www.anekopress.com

Aneko Press, Life Sentence Publishing, and our logos are trademarks of
Life Sentence Publishing, Inc.
203 E. Birch Street
P.O. Box 652
Abbotsford, WI 54405

JUVENILE FICTION / Religious / Christian / Action & Adventure

Paperback ISBN: 979-8-88936-294-4

eBook ISBN: 979-8-88936-295-1

10 9 8 7 6 5 4 3 2 1

Available where books are sold

CONTENTS

CHAPTER 1

A KNOCK AT THE DOOR

Felicia Cartright and Joan Bailey stood before the narrow window of the rambling adobe house in Mexico, watching the heat shimmer relentlessly on the graveled walk. Felicia's small face was flushed and moist with perspiration, and her body ached with fatigue.

"I don't want anyone to tell me that it gets hot back at Wellington," Joan murmured. "Ever!"

"Ed says it will be cooler after sundown," Felicia said.

Her best friend sighed wearily. "That's good news!"

The girls turned their attention toward the window once more. The sun was about to give up its fierce, unequal battle for a few, brief hours and drop behind the mountain peaks to rest. Only a sliver of fire tinted the western horizon, but July's hot, dusty breath still lingered in the valley.

In spite of the heat, Felicia and Joan were fascinated by the scene. Strange, forbidding shadows wrapped themselves around the ruins of the town of Alamos in southern Sonora, Mexico; a shroud to hide the shame and desolation of the once proud little community. The girls watched intently, for twilight lasted only a moment before giving way to the night. The bells, high atop the spire of the town's only church, pealed out mournfully to signal the passing of another day.

It was as though the girls had stepped into a new and different world they had only vaguely known existed a short time before. It was a hot, dirty, poverty-stricken world that sapped at their strength and tugged at their heartstrings.

Even as they watched, a ragged Indian and his wife, old before their time and their faces set stoically against the hardness of their lot, plodded past. Their pace was slow and shuffling, the resignation of a lifetime of hunger and self-denial in every movement. The Indian couple turned off the street and began to thread their way up the narrow, twisted path.

Neither girl spoke until the couple passed out of view.

"Don't you feel sorry for them?" Felicia asked. "They seem so desolate."

"It's no wonder that Nina Bauer, the girl we met on the plane, came down here to be a missionary," Joan said impulsively. "Just seeing these people makes me want to be the same."

Felicia Cartright exhaled.

"I'm glad Uncle Art asked us to come down here for him," she said. "I'd never have believed what it's like without seeing it. So beautiful, but with such a need for the gospel of Jesus Christ."

Joan glanced over her shoulder to be sure that they were alone.

"Did you find out what that thing we brought down here is for?" she whispered. "Or why it couldn't have been sent by mail?"

Felicia wiped the perspiration from her forehead. At the time Uncle Art had asked her if they would make the trip, it had seemed a normal enough request. Fly down to Mexico with the instrument for Ed, visit him and his two children for a couple of weeks, and go back to Wellington School for Girls in New England.

It had only been that morning, but it seemed an eon or two since they left Dallas by plane for the obscure, mountain village in Mexico.

"We brought Ed a mineral light," Felicia answered in an undertone. "At least that's what Uncle Art called it. He said it was something Ed needed in his prospecting. I think he actually planned on bringing it himself until he got so busy at the plant."

"I know all that," Joan countered, "but what is a mineral light? And why did it have to be delivered in person?"

They were talking softly but were so engrossed

they didn't hear Ed Collins come up behind them, leaning heavily on his cane, until he spoke.

"There is a reason why we couldn't risk having the mineral light come down by mail," he said.

The sound of his voice startled them, and they turned quickly.

"There's a very good reason," he went on.

A smile came to rest briefly on his lips.

"I'm on the trail of something," he said. As he spoke, he subconsciously lowered his voice. "Something that could be mighty big if it proves out."

"You mean you're about to find a mine?" Joan asked excitedly.

"Let's say that I'm about to find a vein of ore," he corrected her. "Or that we hope to find one. At this point, there's no knowing whether it will ever prove out or not."

"That is exciting," Felicia said.

"In more ways than you can imagine," her cousin answered laconically.

He lowered himself to a straight-backed chair and looked at them amiably.

"You've got to understand this country and the Americans who come down here," he continued. "They're mostly a greedy, desperate lot. They'd do anything to steal a man's claim if they thought he had latched on to something."

Felicia's lips parted, and she moistened them with the tip of her tongue.

"Is that why you had us bring the mineral light?" she asked.

"Exactly. You see, a mineral light is used for detecting certain kinds of minerals. Some minerals fluoresce, or shine, under ultraviolet light. A mineral light gives off ultraviolet, or black light. By shining it on rock specimens, certain types of ore can be detected."

The girls moved closer.

"That sounds exciting," Joan said.

"Can we help you?" Felicia wanted to know.

He shook his head.

"I don't think I'm going to be able to do very much," he said, glancing down at his leg. "I suppose I'll have to take it easy for a month or so."

Joan's face revealed her disappointment.

Just then Sue Collins came to the kitchen door.

"Dad," she called, smiling, "dinner is ready."

"Oh, Sue!" Felicia exclaimed, turning. "I'm so sorry we left you to do all the work. We got so interested in looking out the window that we forgot about eating and everything else."

"That's all right," her cousin's daughter said. "There's no use in both of us risking heat prostration out here. Besides, everything's ready."

"Joan and I will do the dishes," Felicia told her.

They sat down at the table.

"Where's Tim?" Joan asked, looking around.

"Oh, he'll be along shortly!" Ed replied. "He knows

when we eat. If he isn't here on time, he has to fend for himself."

He picked up a plate of cold meat and passed it to Felicia.

For a brief instant, she stared at him.

"Is there something wrong?" he asked.

"Not exactly," she replied hesitantly, "only we're used to asking the blessing before we eat." Then, realizing she may have been rude, she said quickly, "I'm sorry for speaking out like that. I didn't mean to be rude, and I certainly didn't want to criticize you."

"That's quite all right, Felicia. I guess I should have remembered that your whole family was religious. Would you say grace?"

She prayed a short prayer, asking God's blessing on each one of them and on the food they were about to eat.

When she looked up, she saw that Sue was studying her intently. Although Sue was her second cousin, they were about the same age. Sue stood half a head taller than Felicia. Her brown hair was bleached by the same sun that had dyed her skin a deep olive through long months of exposure. But she was an attractive girl, a striking girl of the sort one did not soon forget.

"Did you try the mineral light, Dad?" Sue asked after a time.

He shook his head.

"Haven't had a minute," he told her. "But I thought

we'd all go out and see how it works as soon as we finish dinner."

Sue went to the kitchen for more tea.

"I still can't figure out what happened to your old one," she said when she returned. "I thought you practically never lost anything."

"You're right, Kitten," he told her, laying aside his fork. "You're absolutely right."

A strange look came to her eyes.

"But I thought–" she began hesitantly.

"That I'd lost it?" He shook his head. It's gone all right, but I didn't lose it." There was a strange tone in his voice.

Sue's eyes widened.

"You mean that somebody stole it?" she echoed.

"I thought you knew that, Kitten," he said. "I remember very distinctly putting it back in the case and stowing it away in the jeep. But when I unloaded the next morning, it was gone."

"Couldn't it have jostled out?" she asked incredulously.

"I wish I could believe that," he said. "It would make our problems now so much simpler."

Felicia and Joan were staring at one another, questions in their eyes.

"But if you had one mineral light," Joan asked, "and it was stolen, what difference would it make if you bought another and had it sent to you by mail?"

Ed lowered his voice.

"It probably does sound silly to you," he said, his gray eyes intense, "but I just don't dare risk it. If people saw me getting a package right after my mineral light was stolen, they would know I was on to something that made me need one badly."

"But why?" Felicia asked. "Don't most prospectors use them?"

"Not when they're as hard up as I am," he said. "At least, I wouldn't be expected to buy a new one right away unless I thought I had to have it."

"And you figure that by not sending for one you'll be able to do a better job of throwing these people, whoever they are, off the track," Joan ventured. "Is that it?"

"Exactly."

"Just what is it you expect to find?" Felicia asked. She realized the instant she asked that she shouldn't have. The warning signals went up in her cousin's eyes.

"A secret you don't know is an easy one to keep," he told them.

"Oh, Dad!" Sue broke in. "Aren't you going to tell us?"

There was a sharp knock at the door.

Joan straightened and caught her breath. "W-w-who's that?" she demanded. "Tim?"

Sue shook her head.

"It wouldn't be him," she said. "He wouldn't knock!"

CHAPTER 2

JUMPY!

For the space of a heartbeat, conversation in the heat-choked living room ceased. Felicia glanced questioningly at her cousin. He cleared his throat and reached for his cane.

"I–I'll go to the door," he said. He seemed to falter momentarily.

"I'll go, Dad!" Sue exclaimed, getting to her feet and running lightly across the floor.

The knock came again. This time it was hesitant, almost fearful.

Sue opened the door.

"Good evening," she said. Her voice was cordial enough, but there was a question in her tone.

"Is–is this the Collins' residence?" a girl's voice asked tremulously, "the place where Felicia Cartright and Joan–Joan Bailey are staying?"

"Nina Bauer!" Felicia cried excitedly as she hurried to the door.

Joan was also leaving the table when Ed Collins stopped her with a glance.

"A friend of yours, Joan?" he asked, his voice soft but edged with steel.

She nodded.

"We met her on the plane coming down," she whispered. "She's a missionary going to a station north of here."

There was a strange look in his eyes. "Are you sure?"

"Of course. Why would she lie about a thing like that?"

He did not answer her question. "You didn't tell her about the mineral light, did you?" he asked instantly. "You didn't mention what I do?"

"We might have," Joan replied. "I don't remember."

"Joan!" Felicia called just then. "Do you know who's here?"

Joan joined the girls at the door.

Nina Bauer was standing just inside the door. The feeble light bulb in the lamp was just bright enough to reveal the softness of her auburn hair and the delicate cut of her features.

Ed Collins got to his feet painfully and hobbled into the room. He picked up a magazine with exaggerated carelessness and leafed the pages. But for all his studied indifference, his eyes were stealthily appraising the newcomer.

She was a pretty girl. There was no mistaking that, well-mannered and gracious. Her eyes were brown, or were they hazel? She was older than Felicia and Joan by several years but had something of the same look about her. A gentleness that spoke of both refinement and honesty.

But that didn't matter. It was her reason for coming to them that counted. The real reason, not necessarily the one she was giving.

"I'm terribly embarrassed at coming to beg for help," she said, "but frankly, I'm desperate. I'm afraid the mission didn't get my letter that I would be able to come a month earlier as they asked me to."

Ed Collins lifted his eyebrows.

"What makes you think that?" he asked.

Felicia glanced at him quickly. The tone in his voice was so–so caustic. But if the missionary noticed it, she gave no sign.

"I checked at the airport," she went on, "and at the hotel, but there was no word for me. And they said they would meet me."

"Won't you come in and sit down?" Sue asked. "I'm sorry we've kept you standing like this for so long."

Her dad frowned at her but did not speak until they were seated.

Nina Bauer folded her small hands on her lap.

"It's awfully presumptuous of me to come here like this," she said, "but I don't know another person here in Alamos."

"Are you sure?" Collins blurted.

Nina started at the accusation in his voice.

"Dad!" Sue chided. "Of course, she's sure that she doesn't know anyone else here in Alamos. How could she? She only came in this afternoon."

Nina Bauer's face was white, and her lips were trembling. She moved as though to go.

"Don't leave!" Sue protested. "Please!" She cast a hurt, pleading look at her father, asking him, wordlessly, to do something. "Dad didn't mean anything by it. Honestly."

"I'm awfully sorry," he told her. He smiled impulsively. "But after you are out here for a while, you get so wary you don't trust anybody."

"I–I came to Felicia and Joan," the missionary went on in a small, faltering voice, "because they are Christians, and they were coming here to visit you, and–" her voice trailed off into silence.

"Just where is this mission you're going to?" he asked. His voice was relaxed now and believing.

"It's somewhere north of here," Nina answered uncertainly. "I have the name of the place here."

She showed him a letter.

"I know the place well," he said. "I've done a lot of prospecting all through that Yaqui River territory."

Some of the tenseness left her face.

"Could you tell me how to get there?" she asked. "I don't have too much money, but I could pay."

"We'll do better than that," he replied. "We'll take you there tomorrow or the next day."

"You will?" Her entire being brightened for an instant. "But I couldn't let you go to all that trouble."

"Let us worry about trouble," he went on. "Sue and I will have to take the girls out in the hills and show them this Mexico of ours sooner or later. We'd just as well get it over with. Besides, I imagine they'll enjoy visiting a mission station."

"Oh, we will!" they chorused. "We'll love it."

Nina's eyes grew wide and luminous. "I don't know how I can ever thank you."

"Don't," he told her with a gruffness that was belied by the twinkling of his eyes, "it will only embarrass both of us."

She rose to leave.

"My cab is still waiting," she said.

"Why don't you stay here with us?" Sue asked her. "We have plenty of room."

"Thank you," the missionary girl answered, "but I've already checked in at the hotel, and my things are all there."

In a moment or two she was gone.

"I suppose dinner is cold," Ed Collins grumped as soon as the door closed behind her. "We'd better get back to the table."

Sue came up behind him and kissed him on the forehead. "Oh, Daddy," she said, "you're a darling!"

"I only did what you wanted me to," he retorted. "Figured if I didn't, I'd never hear the last of it."

"It is awfully nice of you, Ed," Felicia told him. "Nina told us on the plane that she only had a few dollars left after buying her ticket."

He put a spoonful of sugar into his tea and stirred it vigorously.

"I only hope she's everything she says she is," he murmured.

"Oh, Dad! You're so suspicious lately. It's a wonder you even trust Tim and me."

"I know that both you and Tim laugh at me for being jumpy," he said, "but I tell you, there's something to be jumpy about." He leaned forward and lowered his voice. "I didn't tell you this before, Sue, because I didn't want to worry you. But my climbing rope didn't *break,* causing me to fall last week."

Felicia and Joan started, and Sue gasped involuntarily. "What do you mean?" she asked.

"My climbing rope didn't break, Susan," he repeated. *"It was cut!"*

"But why?" she persisted. "What would make anyone do a thing like that?"

"It's like I've been telling you," he whispered. "Someone else is after the same vein of ore I'm after, and they're afraid I'm going to find it first!"

The silence in the stifling, little room was deafening.

CHAPTER 3

TURN OFF THE LIGHT!

They were still sitting at the table when the kitchen door opened and Tim came sauntering in.

"Tim!" Sue called out. "Look who's here."

He came into the dining room, grinning broadly.

"Hi, Felicia!" he said. "I see you made it."

He was about her age or a little older. His face was lean and hard and tanned to a leather-brown by the merciless sun. He was not particularly tall but was compactly built. His years of football were revealed in his powerful shoulders and the quick, catlike way in which he walked.

Felicia introduced him to Joan.

"Hello," he said, smiling easily. And then, just remembering, he turned to his father. "By the way, Dad, Pietro and that pal of his, Juan whatever-his-name-is, are at the back door."

"Why didn't you tell me?" Ed pushed back from the table. "Have them come in."

The boy hesitated.

"They're awfully dirty. They've been in the hills for a week."

Ed grasped the table and would have stood, but Sue spoke quickly.

"Have them come in, Tim. That won't make any difference."

Her brother laughed.

"Tender-hearted Sue," he chided. There was a trace of pride in his voice. "It's the heat, Felicia. She's been down here so long she's going soft."

Nevertheless, he went out and called to the two men.

"Come on in, Pietro," he said. "Dad will talk to you inside."

"*Sí*, Tim," a liquid, musical voice answered. "*Gracias.*"

"These men are Dad's Indian prospectors," Sue whispered in explanation. "He has them go out into the hills and do a lot of the leg work. Then if they come up with something that looks promising, he goes out and checks further. It saves him a great deal of time."

But Felicia and Joan were scarcely listening. Pietro and Juan had come into the kitchen. Juan was short and stocky, his features coarse and his face as inscrutable as the hills they had just left. His mouth was in a perpetual frown. But Pietro was the opposite. He was as tall as his companion was short. Tall and dark and regal in build and manner.

It was obvious that he was the leader of the two.

"How did it go, Pietro?" Ed asked.

The Indian moved silently to the kitchen table and emptied a small leather pouch of ore samples on it. The girls entered the kitchen and looked on curiously.

"Is there anything here that looks good?" Ed repeated.

"Maybe," Juan broke in, shrugging his shoulders. "Who knows?"

Pietro glared at him.

"No," he said quickly. "Nothing of good."

Ed picked up a piece of ore and examined it critically. "Copper," he mused. "Did you mark the spot where you found it?"

"*Si.*" Pietro took a greasy map from his pocket and spread it before the prospector. "We got samples from here – and here – and here." He shook his head. "But we got nothing of good. Nothing of good."

Ed nodded.

"Low-grade copper ore," he said. "Probably not worth checking out." He looked up, and when he spoke again, it was with affected carelessness. "Did you see anyone else prospecting while you were out?" he asked.

It seemed to Felicia that Pietro started to shake

his head once more, but Juan spoke quickly, blurting the words.

"*Sí,*" he said. "We see a man with the box that makes the funny light. You know, the box like you lose that time. We see him. He go along at night. But we no see what he find."

Ed Collins started slightly.

"Was it Martin Spanner?" he asked.

Pietro bristled. "Not close enough to see. It was only one time we get look at him, and only for a minute. When he see us, he run back to his horse and ride off fast."

"Maybe he's the guy who stole my mineral light," Ed observed.

Juan turned to him. "You get another box that makes the rocks shine?" he asked curiously. "You get another one soon?"

The prospector did not answer him.

"Sue," he said, glancing up at his daughter, "get Pietro and Juan their wages."

He counted the money out to the men, peso by peso. They accepted it silently and turned to go.

"*Gracias,*" Pietro muttered. "*Gracias, Señor.*"

When they were gone, Sue shuddered.

"I don't know why it is," she said, "but I don't trust those men."

"You were the one who insisted on inviting them in," her brother told her. "Remember?"

"We've got to be nice to them," she said defensively.

"Pietro and Juan are all right," their dad said. He had picked up the ore samples and was examining them again carefully. "You can't exactly blame them for acting as they do. Some of the Americans who have come down here have treated them and their people so shamefully." He turned to Tim. "Have they gone yet?"

The boy moved to the window, pulled the curtain back slightly, and looked out.

"I don't see any sign of them," he said.

"We'll wait a few more minutes," Ed went on. "They might still be hanging around outside. I want to try out that new mineral light and see if it's any good."

Tim Collins' eyes lit up. "Did you get the light, Felicia?" he asked excitedly.

"Yes," she said.

"Why else do you think they came down?" Sue asked him.

"Oh, I don't know!" he answered, grinning. "I thought maybe they'd heard about me and figured they had to come down and have a look."

Sue made a wry face at him.

"Why don't you get the mineral light, Sue?" Ed Collins asked. "I don't know whether there's anything in these samples to show how it works, but we ought to get something."

Felicia joined Sue.

"I'll go with you," she said. "I have the instrument in my suitcase."

In a moment they were back with it.

Ed Collins took the mineral light from its case and looked at it approvingly. "Leave it to Dad," he said. "Ask him to get something and he always gets the best there is on the market."

Tim picked up the ore and looked at it.

"You don't think there's anything in this, do you?" he asked doubtfully. "I don't think we'll get any fluorescence at all."

"We'll soon know," his father said. "Turn off the light, will you, Joan? The switch is right behind you."

She turned off the light, and their host moved the small black box slowly over the ore samples on the table. The first piece or two revealed nothing at all, and Tim laughed.

"See," he said, "what did I tell you? There's not a trace of light."

"But look now," Sue countered loyally. "You can see little flecks of something in that piece."

"Is that what you're looking for?" Felicia asked curiously.

"Not exactly," her cousin answered. "That is the way the mineral light works all right, but we'd have to find a much greater show than there is here in order to make an ore sample interesting."

"What metal is that, Dad?" Tim asked.

"Here's a piece down by my foot," Sue broke in. "Why don't you try it?"

She laid it on the table, and her dad passed the mineral light over it.

There was a sudden burst of light, dancing like fire from a thousand pinpoints on the ore sample.

Joan gasped.

Ed Collins brought the mineral light back over the ore sample and held it there. The entire rock seemed alive with light.

For a minute, no one in the little group moved or spoke. They could not. The little machine had caught them and held them captive.

Felicia's heart was beating faster, and perspiration dotted her forehead. She wiped it away with trembling fingers and shifted uncertainly from one foot to the other. In the faint light of the moon that shone through the window, Felicia could make out the figures of her companions and the outline of the mineral light. It was shaking in Ed Collins' hands and he was breathing heavily.

"What is it, Dad?" Tim asked. Although he scarcely spoke above a whisper, his voice sounded harsh and as booming as a cannon.

"I–I'm not sure," Ed replied. It was as though he stood a mile away, his voice was so distant and expressionless. "It could be a number of things."

He switched off the mineral light. "Turn on the lights, somebody."

Joan turned quickly and fumbled for the toggle.

The light bulb glowed weakly and scarcely dispelled

the shadows in the corners of the room, but for an instant, the tense little group stared at one another numbly. It all seemed so strange, so unreal.

Felicia Cartright was staring at the ore sample on the table. It looked ordinary enough. It couldn't be so valuable.

"What do you think it is?" Tim insisted.

Ed Collins expelled his breath slowly, as though with great effort. He picked up the ore, examined it with loving fingers, and returned it to the table gently, as though the slightest jar might cause it to disappear.

The girls were leaning forward intently, waiting for him to speak.

"I'd rather not say right now," he continued after what seemed to be a long time but was probably less than a minute. "But if it's what I think it is, we've got the best chance of making a rich strike that we've had in the eighteen years I've been grubbing around these hills."

"We can get the assayer to look at it tonight," Tim suggested, his voice rising. "I've gotten him out at night before this. He'd know what it is. Or we could get Doc Wimberly to tell us. He's a graduate geologist. He'd know if anyone would."

His dad shook his head.

"We're not to breathe a word of this to anyone," he said. "Understand?"

"But we've *got* to find out what it is."

"We'll find out," Ed went on. "Get me a hammer, Tim, and that piece of iron out by the back step."

Tim did as he was told.

Spreading a paper under the iron, Ed laid the ore on it, broke off a piece, and crushed it methodically. Tim's face was ashen, and his mouth twitched nervously as he watched his dad work. Joan swallowed hard.

"T-t-this suspense is getting me," she muttered to no one in particular.

Ed Collins, who had not spoken since he started to work, was shaking as he pulverized the rock.

"The pie tin, Sue," he said curtly, sounding more like a surgeon ordering his nurse in surgery than a prospector.

She got the pie tin. He scooped the powder into it and moved to the sink, where he washed it with water the way the early prospectors used to pan for gold. The girls and Tim crowded closely around him.

In a minute or two, a fine, white powder settled to the bottom of the tin. He cried out exultantly.

"See that!" he shouted. "See that!"

"I still don't know what it is," Tim said.

Ed Collins switched off the ceiling bulb and groped for the mineral light. It was a moment or two before he managed to train the ultraviolet beam from the mineral light on the white powder in the pan. It glowed and sparkled like a thousand diamonds twinkling in the sun.

"Ohl" Felicia gasped.

"Scheelite!" Ed announced triumphantly. "It's that find of scheelite we've been after for the past six months."

For a time, Ed kept the mineral light trained on the pan, watching the dancing light with strange fascination.

"Are you sure it's scheelite, Dad?" Tim asked. "You couldn't be making a mistake, could you?" Suddenly he sounded weak and far away, as one whose mind is going blank before fainting.

Ed Collins turned on the light again and went back to the kitchen table where he sat down once more, heavily.

"I suppose I could be making a mistake," he said. "There's a good deal about prospecting and ores that I don't know. But I'd stake any reputation I might have that this is scheelite."

"But what's it for?" Joan asked brashly. "I don't think I ever heard of it before."

"I thought I told you about it at the table," he replied.

"All you said was that you were on to something that could be an important find for someone."

"I didn't plan to tell you, but since I've gone this far, I guess I'd just as well. Scheelite is the substance that tungsten is found in. I've known there was a big concentration of it somewhere close. We kept getting traces of it along the river, as though it had washed downstream. But we didn't find it in anything approaching paying quantities."

"Is that what you were talking about when you ordered that first mineral light?" Sue asked. "You kept telling us that you were finding something that might be big."

He nodded. "I wasn't sure that we were running across scheelite, but I had a good hunch that it was. Then when we got the first mineral light, I knew that's what we were finding when I crushed some ore samples. But we've never run across anything to compare with this."

"Where did it come from?" Sue asked.

"That's easy," her brother answered. "All we've got to do is check Pietro's map, and we'll have it. There aren't over three or four places to check out."

"But I picked this piece of ore off the floor," Sue reminded him. "It could have been something that was brought in weeks ago."

Ed Collins stared at her. "I'd never thought of that!" he exclaimed.

CHAPTER 4

A FACE AT THE WINDOW

Tim Collins picked up the ore next, turning it in his stubby, calloused fingers.

"This piece was found in a river or creek," he announced after a time. "You can see the action of the water on it. It's been worn smooth."

"I noticed that," his dad said. "Get Pietro's map, and let's have a look at it. Maybe that will tell us something."

Tim spread the heavy, greasy paper on the table before them and pointed to the crude X marks the Indian had made.

"There are his marks," he said. "They're all three on creek beds."

Ed nodded in agreement. "That means it could have been found in any one of those spots or none of them." Again, he examined the bit of ore. "We know this much. It has been in the water a long while. Even if we find out for sure where he got the ore, we won't know definitely whether it actually originated there or tumbled to the place from some spot up stream."

"At least we have something to go on," Tim replied, his youthful face tense with emotion.

"We'll go and talk with Pietro and Juan in the morning," his dad said. "Maybe we can learn something more from them."

"What about Nina Bauer?" Sue asked, suddenly remembering the missionary who had been at the house earlier in the evening.

"What about her?" Tim demanded.

"We promised to take her up to the mission station in the morning," Sue said. "She'll be counting on us."

"And we'll do just that, Kitten," Ed answered.

"But, Dad!" her brother protested. "We can't let a thing like that interfere with our getting out to hunt for this ore. We've got to make every minute count. Someone else might beat us to it."

"Did you notice where Pietro and Juan were prospecting this week?" Ed asked him. "They were in the hills north of Alamos. We can take her to the mission at the same time we go prospecting. In fact, it might be a good blind to cover up what we're really doing to have the girls along."

"You don't have to take us, Ed," Felicia told him quickly. "We don't want to get in your way. We can take care of ourselves while you're gone."

The corners of his mouth tightened.

"I suppose we'd better wait until after we talk with Pietro in the morning," he said, "to see whether the terrain is too difficult for you to make it comfortably. If it isn't, there's no reason why we can't all go together if you want to."

"If we want to?" Joan echoed. "It sounds wonderful!"

"Well, I think we'd all better get to bed," he suggested. "We'll have to be getting up early in the morning."

"I don't think I'll be able to close my eyes all night," Tim said.

"You'd better," his dad answered. "We may have a rugged day tomorrow and a good many rugged days following tomorrow."

Soon Joan and Felicia were in their small bedroom together.

"Isn't this exciting?" Felicia whispered as soon as the door closed behind them. "Oh, I hope we get to go along!"

"So do I."

"Because of the prospecting?" Felicia asked. Her face was serious, but her eyes were dancing. "Or because of Tim?"

"Felicia!" Joan gasped.

"I saw you watching him. If we hadn't had the lights out when Ed turned the mineral light out, I don't think either one of you would have seen the reaction the ultraviolet rays showed." She laughed.

"In fact, every time Tim looked at you, Joan, you glowed just like that rock did under the mineral light."

"Felicia!" Joan warned. "If you weren't my best friend, I'd–"

Felicia dropped to a chair beside the bed and began to take off her shoes.

"Aren't they the nicest people?" she asked. "Seriously, I mean."

Her friend eyed her critically to be sure that it wasn't another joke. "I couldn't help thinking the same thing myself when your cousin said he would still take Nina out to the mission station, in spite of this important new ore."

"They're so nice," Felicia repeated, "and yet they don't see that they have any need for the Lord Jesus as their Savior. They don't drink or smoke or swear. Ever since Ed's wife died three years ago, he's been both father and mother to the kids, and they get along well together."

Joan was silent for a moment or two.

"I suppose they would be just about the hardest kind of people to talk with about Christ," she said, "because they live such good, moral lives. They would be terribly hard to convince that they need a Savior."

Felicia picked up her Bible and opened it to the place where they had been reading for devotions.

"Mom says that has been the stumbling block for her brother, Ed's dad, and the entire family for twenty-five or thirty years," she continued. "They're good people, and everybody likes and respects them. They seem to have the idea that they are so good they don't need Jesus."

"And that's probably one of the biggest sins of all," Joan answered, "to put our trust for salvation in our own righteousness when the Bible tells us that we aren't righteous in God's sight at all."

They had their devotions together and got into bed. For several minutes they lay there in the darkness.

"Felicia," Joan whispered sometime later, "are you still awake?"

The other girl rolled over and mumbled something unintelligibly.

"Felicia, I want to talk to you."

"About Tim?"

"No, silly!" Joan countered. "I just remembered something. It–it may be important."

Felicia raised on one elbow. "Don't tell me that you left the water running in our room back at school. They'll have a terrible water bill by the time we get back in the fall."

"Felicia! This is serious!" Joan Bailey sat upright in bed. "It was something I saw tonight just after I turned out the light so your cousin could examine the ore samples with his new mineral light." She paused. "I happened to glance out the window as I turned back after the light was out."

"Yes?"

"And I saw an Indian walking by!"

"No!" Felicia exclaimed. "You must have been mistaken."

"I wasn't mistaken. If I close my eyes, I can still see him." She shuddered. "I don't know whether he was walking away from the house, just going past, or whether he was slipping back to look in on us."

"Why didn't you say something about it?" her companion wanted to know.

"Just then everybody got so excited about the ore we were examining," she said, "that I forgot all about it. And I didn't remember it again until right now."

In spite of herself, Felicia felt the color drain from her cheeks. "Was it one of the Indians who were in the house?" Felicia asked. "Or could you tell?"

"I just don't know," she answered. "It was dark outside, and I couldn't see the man's face. He wasn't too big. At least I don't think he was. I don't know what was wrong with me that I didn't take a closer look or at least tell someone about it."

The clock in the living room struck eleven. Neither girl spoke until the last chime died away.

"What do you suppose we ought to do about it?" Felicia asked. "Tell Ed?"

"I wonder if it would do any good to tell him about it tonight," Joan said. "It was almost two hours ago."

"I suppose it wouldn't. The guy isn't there still. We know that. And I heard Ed and Tim go through the house checking the doors and windows after we went to bed. They aren't taking any chances."

Joan sprang to her feet. "That reminds me!" she exclaimed. "We haven't checked to see that our windows are locked."

A moment later she returned to the bed.

"I declare," she said, "I don't know what's the matter with me. I'm getting as nervous and worried about things as my grandma."

"You can always shout for Tim," Felicia reminded her, "if you get scared or think you're in danger."

"In case you're interested," Joan said, "I'm sticking my tongue out at you."

Felicia closed her eyes. "I suppose it's just as well to wait until morning to tell Ed what you saw," she said, changing the subject.

The following morning, shortly after daylight, there was a sharp rap on their door.

"Felicia!" Tim called. "Joan! It's time to hit the deck! Breakfast is about ready!"

"In the middle of the night?" Joan Bailey complained.

"Listen, girl!" he informed her. "We get up in the morning around here. Let's get with it!"

They scrambled out of bed and, in a few moments, were dressed and in the kitchen.

Hurriedly, Joan told Ed Collins and Tim what she had seen the night before.

Ed tugged at his chin thoughtfully. "That could mean a great deal," he said, "or it could mean nothing.

Everyone is more or less informal out here. It could be that someone was taking a shortcut to his home."

Tim pulled up a chair and sat down. "We've got other things to think about right now," he said. "What do you figure we ought to do the first thing this morning, Dad?"

Ed spoke slowly.

"I gave it a lot of thought last night," he said. "I don't believe we ought to tell Pietro and Juan about our find. I'm not sure that we can depend entirely on them."

"But we'll give them their cut if we make a strike, won't we?" Tim asked.

"Of course," his dad replied quickly. "I wouldn't think of doing anything else. But I don't want them to let word slip and find out later that someone else has beaten us to it because of them. That won't do any of us any good."

"How do you figure on getting that info," Tim continued, "without spilling everything?"

"You leave that to me," his dad answered, smiling. "Now, what do you say we have breakfast?"

They sat down at the table together. Tim reached for a slice of toast, but his dad stopped him with a glance. They bowed their heads respectfully and waited until after Felicia had prayed.

CHAPTER 5

THE EAVESDROPPER

After breakfast they all piled into the jeep and went across the crumbling town of Alamos to the wretched, little hovel where Pietro lived with his family.

"Well," Ed Collins said, pulling to a stop, "this is where we see whether Pietro knows anything or not."

Joan Bailey blanched.

"Do you mean that people actually live in there?" she asked.

"Actually," Tim told her, "Pietro is better off than many of his tribe. He has a job and a home of his own. It might not be much, but it means everything to him."

Ed got out.

"Do you want to go inside?" he asked. "Or would you rather wait out here?"

Sue turned to Felicia and Joan.

"I wouldn't miss it," Felicia said eagerly.

"You see, that's the trouble with being her friend," Joan said to Sue as she followed the Cartright girl out of the aging vehicle. "She just wouldn't miss *anything*. One of these times she's going to get both of us killed or something."

The tall, dark-skinned Yaqui came to the door. His eyes searched Ed's face intently but without visible emotion. His voice, when he spoke, was flat and colorless.

"You wish to see Pietro, Señor?" he asked.

Something about the Indian's manner disturbed Felicia vaguely. It was certainly not his dark skin or his stilted, clumsy use of English. That she knew. Actually, it was nothing she could pinpoint or find the words to describe. It was a filmy, half-formless impression, an inner feeling that made her cringe and want to get away from him.

"I had a couple of questions I wanted to clear up," Ed said carelessly. "Thought maybe you could help me."

"*Sí.*"

He would have kept them standing at the door if Ed had not asked to go in.

"*Sí,*" he repeated in response to his question, "if you want to." The expression on his swarthy face did not change.

"I'm going to take the girls with me prospecting for a few days," Ed told him. "And we'd like to do some looking around in the places where you got some of those ore samples you brought us last night."

Pietro glanced down at Ed's leg but said nothing.

"Now exactly where did you get them?" Ed asked.

"We gave you the map."

"I know, but I'd like a little more information."

For an instant, but only for an instant, a strange light flickered in the Indian's eyes.

"You get a new mineral light, no?" he asked.

Tim Collins started violently, but Ed's face remained as impassive as the Indian's.

"Did you find this piece on the river?" he asked, holding out a chunk of ore.

A corner had been knocked off it with a hammer, but it was not the piece that contained the scheelite. Felicia saw that at a glance. Pietro held it between thumb and forefinger.

"Maybe," he said. "Maybe no." He handed the ore back to Ed indifferently. "It was marked on the map like you tell us to do."

"You didn't have the ore samples marked this time, Pietro. I'd like to know which came from which spot. Surely you can remember where you got this sample."

"You have the map with you?" Pietro asked.

Ed took it from his bag and spread it out between them. The Indian studied it intently.

"I think maybe we get it here," he said at last, indicating a pencil mark with a dirty finger. "Or maybe it was here." He looked up. "You ask Juan?"

"I'm asking you."

There was a long pause.

"Maybe if I go with you, I could remember," he said. "When I see the place I know it, right off. I never forget if I see the place."

Ed folded the map and returned it to his bag.

"I'll let you know."

When they were outside and in the car, Tim turned to his dad. "What are we going to do now?" he asked "We'll have to let Pietro in on it. We'll have to take him into our confidence and have him take us into the hills and show us where they picked up the ore."

"I'm not so sure," Ed replied. "I want to study this map again. There was something strange about Pietro's actions. He was too eager to go along."

"Maybe he suspects that you're on to something big and he's anxious to get in on it."

Ed started the engine and drove slowly away from the Indian's hut. There was little talking by anyone on the way back to the house.

"I think you'd better tell that missionary friend of yours that we won't be able to leave until tomorrow, Felicia," he said when they pulled up into the yard. "Sue can take you to the hotel to talk to her while Tim and I go over that map again."

"And," Tim cautioned, "whatever you do, don't mention prospecting or the scheelite or anything to anyone. This town is full of rascals who would slit all our throats for a chance at a tenth of what this could be. And," he added, "most of them are Americans."

Sue Collins slipped behind the wheel and drove expertly through the narrow, winding streets toward the hotel.

"I don't know whether I'll even be able to sleep tonight," Joan said. "Imagine people living in a place like Pietro and his family have."

"I keep thinking the same thing," Sue replied. "Sometimes it almost makes me want to be a missionary like Nina, so I can help change that sort of thing."

Felicia looked at her strangely.

"A missionary?" Joan echoed.

"I'd like nothing better than to go into homes like that," she continued, "and clean them up and help the people put up screens and get rid of flies and mosquitoes and the filth they live in."

Felicia half turned in the seat to look at her.

"Sue, is that what being a missionary means to you?" she asked.

The girl's eyes widened. "When I think of missionaries," she went on, "I always think of someone who tries to stop suffering and who teaches the people to be sanitary and to live better lives. To me, that's enough to make it the most important task in the world."

"Those things are all important," Felicia said, "but being a missionary means more than that. Those things are just the byproducts, the things that go along with Christianity."

A question came to Sue's face.

"The chief task of any missionary is to present the claims of Jesus Christ," she continued. "A missionary's purpose is to lead people to Jesus Christ, to get people to forsake their old ways, realize that they are sinners and lost for eternity, and put their trust in Christ to go to heaven. The other things that take place, like better health and sanitation, are just the things that go along with Christianity."

Sue turned a corner and stopped to allow a donkey and a cart to move out of the way.

"That's a strange way of putting it," she answered. "Somehow I've never thought of it quite that way."

She pulled up in front of the hotel and parked.

"I suppose there would have to be some way provided for people who are wicked," she went on, "so they could go to heaven."

She would have gotten out of the car, but neither of her companions made a move.

"The Bible tells us that we all are wicked," Felicia said gently.

"Now that seems to be going a little far," Sue told her testily.

The Cartright girl took a small Bible from her purse and opened it.

"*All have sinned, and come short of the glory of God,*" she read. "*There is none righteous. No not one.*" She flipped the pages with easy familiarity. "*All we like sheep have gone astray; we have turned every one to his own way, and the Lord has laid on him the iniquity of us all.*"

Sue's cheeks blanched slightly.

"And in another place," Joan put in, "we're told that the wages of sin is death."

Sue Collins stiffened.

"I much prefer my own concept of God," she said. "I picture Him as a kind, loving heavenly Father, who loves us far too much to–to do something like that to us."

Felicia nodded understandingly.

"Quite a few people feel that way," she said. "But they don't get it from the Bible, and after all, that's God's Word to us. When it gets right down to it, Sue, it doesn't make too much difference what you believe or what I believe or what someone else believes. The things that really matter are what does the Bible say and what have *you* done with Christ?"

Sue did not move for a moment or two. Then she took the key from the ignition and got out of the car with firm resolution. Felicia and Joan followed her.

Nina Bauer was sitting in the lobby of the hotel, an open Bible on her lap, when they entered. She looked up and smiled.

"Good morning!" Nina closed the Book and got to her feet. "I was just wondering whether we were going this morning or not. I thought you would be here a little earlier if you were going today."

"Right on both counts," Sue answered. It was obvious that she admired and liked the young missionary. "Dad has some things to do today, so he thought we'd better come over and tell you we'll be leaving the first thing in the morning."

The man who was sitting across from them glanced over his paper as she spoke. Felicia's eyes chanced to catch his. They were dark, evil eyes, set in a crinkled, oiled-leather face. He was obviously an American, but he had been burned as dark as any Indian by long periods of exposure to the subtropical sun.

For the space of a heartbeat, his gaze held hers forcibly. Then he smiled and looked away, making no attempt to conceal his interest in what they were saying. Although the grubby, little hotel lobby was already stifling, Felicia shivered as though from the cold.

"Why don't you come out to the house and stay with us tonight?" Sue asked.

Nina shook her head.

"I think it would be better if I stay here," she said. "I don't want to impose on you."

"You won't be imposing."

"Maybe Nina is right," Joan said. "Your dad might prefer not having company right now."

"I don't see why."

This time the eavesdropper lowered his gaze quickly to the paper and kept it there.

"I really think it's better if I stay here, Sue," Nina answered gently. "It's enough that your father has consented to take me out to the mission. I don't want to impose on him."

The girls sat down in the lobby with Nina and visited with her. It was an hour later when Sue glanced at her watch.

"It's almost noon," she exclaimed. "We'll have to run. Dad and Tim will be wondering what happened to us."

They got to their feet and started toward the door.

"I'll see you in the morning," Nina called after them.

When they were outside, Felicia grasped Sue by the arm.

"That man in the hotel," she whispered. "He got up and is following us."

"Are you sure?"

"Let's get out of here quickly," she said. "I don't like this!"

They walked briskly to the car, and Sue pulled out from the curb.

"Turn here," Felicia ordered.

"But that isn't the way home," Sue protested.

"I know it," Felicia replied, "but we've got to lose that man! We can't let him follow us to your home. And the quicker we lose him the better."

CHAPTER 6

AN ODD-SHAPED HOLE!

If the stranger followed them, they were not aware of it. Indeed, it did not seem to Felicia that he could possibly have unraveled all the sharp turns and back-tracking Sue did before starting home.

"I think we've lost him by this time," Joan said, breathing heavily. "Slow down a little, Sue, and give my stomach a chance to catch up."

The young driver laughed nervously.

"I think we've lost him," she said.

Felicia nodded. And then a disturbing thought came to her.

"Oh, Sue!" she exclaimed.

Her cousin stopped suddenly in the middle of the street.

"What's wrong?" she demanded.

"I just thought of something," Felicia went on. "It won't make too much difference if we do lose him.

All he's got to do is talk with Nina. He can pump everything he needs to know from her. And she'd tell him because she doesn't know that there's any reason for not doing so."

Joan Bailey expelled her breath with great deliberation.

"Well," Sue said, starting the engine once more, "there's no point in our sitting here."

When they got back to the house, Ed Collins and Tim were sitting in the living room looking over the map.

"I still think we ought to take Pietro or Juan along," Tim was saying. "He'll remember enough about the terrain and where he picked up the ore to save us a couple of days, or maybe more, even if he didn't remember to mark the samples."

"Could be." Ed Collins tugged at the lobe of his ear thoughtfully. "But I'd still feel better going alone if we think we can manage it. I didn't exactly like the way Pietro acted this morning."

"He's always been reliable before."

"I suppose I'm just jumpy," Ed answered.

"If you'd been with us," Joan broke in, "you'd have something to be jumpy about. Some guy overheard what we were talking to Nina Bauer about and then tried to follow us."

"Are you sure?" Ed demanded.

"What did you tell this Nina Bauer?" Tim wanted

to know. "You didn't mention the scheelite or the mineral light, did you?"

They shook their heads. "We only talked about taking her out to the mission," Sue assured them. "We didn't say a word about prospecting and neither did she."

Tim sighed his relief.

But his father was still disturbed.

"What did this guy look like?" he asked.

Felicia described him as best she could.

Ed laughed mirthlessly. "That description could fit a dozen guys," he said. "And any one of them wouldn't hesitate at anything that would make him a dollar – from larceny to murder."

"But, Dad," Sue protested, "we didn't tell Nina a thing that could have made him or anyone else suspicious."

"I know you didn't, Kitten," he answered, "intentionally. But look at it this way. Those men would never think of going out of their way to do a good turn for anyone. So they would reason that everyone else is the same as they are."

"But I still don't see–" Sue continued.

"I do," Joan broke in. "They would think that the only reason you would go up toward the mission station is because you've found some ore in the area, and you want to have a chance to look at it."

"Exactly," Ed concluded. "And if it's someone who recognized you, or if he's clever enough to talk to Nina and ask her about us, he could soon know about Pietro and Juan and our whole setup." He folded the map once more, nervously, and took it into his den. In a moment, he returned.

"That's one reason I've been hesitant about letting Pietro know too much right now, Tim," he said. "Pietro and Juan have been so shamefully treated by so many Americans that they are resentful and suspicious of all of us. They might be induced to throw in with some scoundrel who wants to jump our claim."

There was a short silence.

"W-w-what can we do?" Felicia asked.

"Right now, the only thing we can do is to go on as though there is nothing wrong and we suspect nothing," Ed told them. "But we'd better keep our eyes open every single minute."

The rest of the day was a busy one. They got their gear together. Tim made arrangements for more horses and then went down to the store to buy supplies for the expedition.

"Well, Dad," he said at the dinner table that evening, "we've got everything ready for tomorrow. All we'll have to do is get into the truck and jeep and head north."

"I haven't thought of anything except that man all day," Sue put in. "Do you suppose he'll really cause us trouble, Dad?"

"Now, Kitten," Ed replied, laughing away her fears, "let's not borrow trouble. It could be that the man wasn't actually listening to you at all, and the chances are that he didn't try to follow you. Maybe we're all a little jumpy and too quick to let our imaginations work overtime."

"Just the same, I'll be glad when we get out in the hills," Tim added.

"Yes," his dad agreed. "I always have felt safer in the hills." He reached for his cane and got slowly to his feet. "I know it's early, but I do think it would be best if we all turn in. We've got a big day coming up tomorrow, and it's going to start at dawn."

"Sounds like a good idea," Joan said. "I'm bushed. But I don't know whether it will do any good for me to go to bed or not. I don't think I'll be able to sleep at all."

"You'll be sawing logs before your head hits the pillow," Felicia told her, "if I know anything about you."

"I know I won't be sleeping tonight," Sue said. "As far as I'm concerned, we'd as well start for the hills right now."

Ed Collins laughed. "Tomorrow you'll be glad you got a night's rest," he said.

They all went to their rooms.

"I'll bet all the doors and windows are locked tonight," Felicia said when they were alone. "I can still see that man in the hotel. I get goose bumps just thinking about him."

Joan went to their window and drew back the shade to be sure the latch was hooked.

"I wonder if our visitor of last night will be around again tonight?" she mused.

"I'd forgotten completely about him," Felicia said.

"I think everybody else has too."

"Are you sure he was an Indian?" Felicia asked. "He might have been our friend from the hotel, you know."

"He was dressed like an Indian. That's all I know." Joan turned quickly. "Let's go out and see if he really was out there last night."

Felicia caught her breath. "I believe you really are serious," she said.

"I've never been more serious in my life." She went to her suitcase and got out a small flashlight. "Now don't make any noise. We don't want the whole household to know what we're doing."

"W-w-what will we do if he's out there now?" Felicia wanted to know.

Joan gulped and swallowed at the lump in her throat that would not go down. "I'd rather not think about that," she said. "That's the sort of thing that bothers my sleep."

She checked the flashlight to be sure it was in working order. "This will only take a minute," she said, "I hope."

They crept stealthily out of their room and through the silent, darkened house to the kitchen door.

"Now where was he?" Felicia whispered when they were out in the warm, night air.

"He must have been standing awfully close to the window," Joan said. "At least let's start to look for footprints there."

"I don't see how we're going to make out anything in this hard ground," Felicia said momentarily. "It's like trying to see a foot imprint on a paved street."

"To tell you the truth," Joan replied, "I don't know whether I really want to see anything or not." Then she noticed the pretty flowers growing beneath the window. "Sue was telling us how she has to water those flowers almost every day in order to keep them alive," she continued. "There's a–"

She never did finish the sentence. As she swung the little finger of light toward the flowers, it came to rest on a huge footprint in the clay at the edge of the flower bed. The sun had baked it almost brick-hard, sharply outlining every detail.

"Felicia," Joan said, "there was a man out here last night. I wasn't imagining it."

"And," the other girl went on, "he was peeking in the window. He wasn't just going by."

Joan moistened her lips nervously. "That means there's a good chance that whoever was out here saw your cousin using the mineral light. Felicia! He could have seen the reaction that piece of ore gave. He could know about the scheelite too!"

Joan turned off the flashlight.

"What are we going to do?" she whispered.

"Let's finish looking at that footprint and get back inside where we belong."

The print was as plain as it had been the minute it was made. Every mark, every nail hole in the heel was visible.

"Did you notice," Felicia asked, "he has a hole in his shoe?"

"If you're through looking, let's–let's get out of here."

They turned and tiptoed back into the house.

"Do you think we ought to wake up your cousin?" Joan asked once they were back in their room with the door closed and bolted.

"We'll tell him about it in the morning," Felicia said. "There's absolutely nothing he can do about it tonight."

"I don't know," Joan said doubtfully. "He could help us with the worrying. That's one thing he could do."

They had their devotions and crawled into bed.

"I'm not going anywhere with you again, Felicia," Joan announced under her breath. "I swear it."

"That's what you said the last time."

Joan rolled over, and, in a moment or two, she was asleep.

Felicia lay beside her for half an hour or more, listening to her friend's slow, rhythmic breathing. What did all this mean? Was someone actually after the claim Ed hoped to find? Or were they just nervous because it was something that could be so big? Felicia closed her eyes, and the next thing she knew it was morning.

Someone was hammering loudly on their door.

"Joan! Felicia! Wake up!"

"What is it?" Joan cried. By this time, she was awake enough to realize that it was Tim who was calling them so excitedly. "Is something wrong?"

"Plenty!" he exclaimed. "The map Pietro gave Dad is gone!"

"Gone!" Joan cried. They both leaped out of bed and scrambled frantically into their robes. "When did it happen?"

Felicia slipped the bolt and swung the door open. Tim's face was an ashen mask, and his eyes were wild and darting.

"We don't know when it happened," he replied. "But it must have been during the night sometime. Dad and I just went into the den to take another look at the map before breakfast when we saw that the place had been broken into and ransacked."

They went with him to the little room on the opposite side of the house.

"I guess it has been broken into!" Felicia said. She was startled to see the condition of the den. Papers were scattered everywhere. File drawers had been jerked out and their contents dumped in a heap on the floor. Desk drawers had been opened and pawed through. Even the wastebasket had been overturned.

"But how did he get in?" Felicia asked incredulously.

Ed Collins, who was searching frantically through the papers, jerked his hand toward the broken window in a hurried gesture.

"I might have known that this old house would be no problem to a thief. I don't suppose that window slowed him up more than a couple of minutes."

"Maybe they weren't looking for the map," Joan said. "After all, nobody knew that you had it. Someone broke in here trying to get your money."

Tim laughed.

"They ought to know better than that. Anyone around Alamos knows that we don't have any money. Not the kind that's worth stealing."

"Tim's right," Ed went on. "This was done by someone who got wind of something and knew how I operate. I mean he could have known that Pietro and Juan always make maps showing the location of every ore sample they pick up. He could have heard that the Indians found something and broke in looking for the map."

"Or he might have seen the scheelite night before last," Joan said. She told them once more about the figure she had seen and that she and Felicia had found a footprint in the flower bed the night before.

Ed nodded. "I saw the same thing yesterday morning," he said, "but I didn't say anything because I didn't think there was any point in worrying you about it."

"Dad," Tim began darkly, "that means there's a good chance someone else knows almost as much about this as we do. If they saw the scheelite react under the mineral light and now they have the map, they can find it as easily as we can."

Ed shook his head.

"We've got to ask Pietro to go along," he said, making up his mind suddenly. "That's our only chance."

They left the house when the sun was just beginning to come over the horizon and drove across Alamos to Pietro's little hut. The big Indian and his family were already up. He invited them inside.

"*Sí,*" he said, sitting down on a rickety chair crossing his legs. "I go with you."

Felicia was staring at the sole of his boot. There was an odd-shaped hole in it. The same shaped hole she and Joan had seen in the footprint outside the window!

Felicia began to tremble and felt the strength leave her body momentarily. At that instant, Joan reached over and squeezed her arm tightly.

She had noticed it too!

CHAPTER 7

THE CHANGED MAP

Felicia and Joan stared at one another and then at Pietro and Ed Collins miserably.

"There isn't a thing we can do," Felicia told herself. "There isn't a single thing we can do."

"When you want to leave?" Pietro asked as casually as though they were talking about a visit to the grocery store or a trip to the service station at the foot of the hill.

"I'd like to have you come back with us now," Ed told him. "We've got to pick up the missionary who's going with us as far as the mission, and then we'll be on our way."

"*Si*" Pietro answered. "We go now."

Felicia caught her cousin's eye and motioned him outside.

"And I thought you ought to know," she whispered

hurriedly, "that his boot is exactly like the footprint we found outside the kitchen window."

"I know," Ed answered blandly.

"You know?" she echoed. "And you're still taking him along with us?"

Her cousin nodded.

"If Pietro is the one Joan saw the other night," he said, "he's just as dangerous away from us as he is with us."

The Indian came to the door and looked out. Ed stopped talking and warned Felicia to silence with his eyes.

"We go now," Pietro said.

Ed Collins turned to his son. "We'll take you and Pietro back to the house to pick up the truck," he said. "Then you can get started while we go over to the hotel and get Nina."

"Where'll we meet?" Tim asked.

"You'd better drive slow enough so we can catch you before you get there," Ed told him. "Pietro will know where to stop, but we won't."

If there was anything disturbing the big Indian, he gave no sign. He sat placidly in the front seat beside Tim, acting as though he did not even hear the conversation that was going on around him.

Ed drove around in back and stopped beside the truck. The horses and gear had already been loaded into it, and the tank was filled with gas.

"I think you're all ready to go," Ed told them.

"Now we'll start north, Dad," Tim repeated, "and expect you to catch us before we get to the turn-off."

Ed Collins nodded.

As soon as Tim and Pietro crawled out, Ed backed the jeep around and headed for the hotel.

"Dad," Sue said, a little catch in her voice, "I'm worried about Tim. Do you think it's safe for him to go out with Pietro alone? After everything that's happened?"

Her father did not answer.

Nina Bauer was waiting for them in the lobby of the hotel, and as soon as the car pulled up to the curb, she came out.

"You'll never know how much I appreciate this," she said, smiling her gratitude. "I'm sure you're an answer to prayer. I was frantic when I learned that there was no one to meet me and there probably wouldn't be anyone in Alamos from the mission for a month."

"We won't be going directly there," Ed said, opening up the back of the car. "Or did I tell you that? We've got a little matter to attend to along the way. But we'll get you there eventually."

He reached to put her suitcase inside but stopped suddenly. His cheeks went a pasty white. His outstretched hand froze where it was, and his eyes grew steel hard.

"Dad!" Sue cried. "What's wrong? What's the matter?"

"What is it, Ed?" Felicia asked.

For answer he reached out and picked up a heavy, folded paper.

"What is it?" Sue demanded.

"Here is that map we thought was stolen," he told them.

"But did you have it out here?" Joan wanted to know. "I thought you put it in the den."

He unfolded the map and glanced at it quickly.

"It's the same one, all right."

Felicia saw that people on the street were staring curiously at Ed. She got out and went back to him.

"Ed," she whispered, "maybe we'd better do our looking somewhere else where we don't have so many spectators."

He glanced up.

"I'd never thought of that," he said. He was obviously flustered. "I don't mind telling you that this has got me flustered." He refolded the greasy map hurriedly and stuffed it into his pocket.

Once they were all in the car, he pulled away from the curb and headed for the highway that led north. For almost ten minutes he did not speak.

"Did anyone ask you any questions about us yesterday morning, Nina?" Felicia asked. "After we were talking with you, I mean."

The missionary pursed her lips. "No one except that man who was sitting there," she said. "He wanted to know if you were tourists and where you were staying."

"That's just what you were afraid of, Dad," Sue broke in.

"Did he say what his name was?" Ed asked.

"No," she answered. "Is there something wrong? Did I do something I shouldn't have done?"

"Of course not," Ed Collins said. "You couldn't have known. Perhaps you had better tell her what this is about, Sue."

Quickly his daughter outlined everything that had happened.

"Oh, I'm sorry I said anything!" she replied.

"He'd probably have found out anyway," Ed answered. "And, of course, he might just have been wanting to make conversation. We might be too suspicious."

That possibility caused Sue to relax a little, but Felicia still felt a heaviness within. That guy was more than casually interested. That much was sure. She had seen that in his eyes.

"I've finally decided one thing," Ed announced suddenly. "We're going to the mission first."

"You won't have to do that on my account, Mr. Collins," Nina told him. "I don't want to cause you any more trouble than I already have."

"It's not that," Ed went on. "The way things are going, I'd better get you and the girls up to the mission before Tim and Pietro and I go into the hills. They'd be welcome to stay there a few days, wouldn't they?"

"I'm sure they would."

"But, Dad!" Sue protested. "You can't do that! We want to go with you."

They were out on the highway now, driving at the legal speed Imit.

"I know," he said, "and I'd like to take you. I know Felicia and Joan would enjoy getting a taste of our kind of life in the hills, but too much has happened to make me feel concerned about this trip. I think Tim and I had better go on alone."

"You want to go along, don't you?" Sue asked Felicia and Joan.

Joan laughed nervously. "Right now, I think I do," she said, "but if something begins to happen, I wonder if I'll be quite so brave."

"Exactly," Felicia's cousin answered. "I'd never forgive myself if I took the four of you along and something happened. We'll go on up to the mission tonight, and Tim, Pietro, and I will head back the first thing in the morning. You can stay there while we're gone. It probably won't be more than a week."

"But, Dad, you'll be delayed another day."

He nodded.

"That's a chance we have to take."

They drove on for several miles in silence.

After a time, Ed took the map from his pocket and handed it back to Felicia.

"Why don't you girls take a look at that?" he asked. "It just occurred to me that those X marks weren't in the places Tim and I thought they were. I was either mistaken just now or he and I misread it."

They unfolded the map and began to study it carefully as Ed Collins drove over the jouncing road.

"What is it you want to know?" Felicia asked.

"How far is the closest X to the mission station?"

"It looks quite a ways," she said. "It's south and quite a long way east of the mission."

He pursed his lips. "That's strange."

"It will be too far to take us over there, Dad," Sue said. "Besides, we won't be any trouble. We can cook for you and–"

"Now, Kitten," he said laughing. "You know that isn't the reason I want to have you stay there."

As they negotiated a sharp corner, he slammed on the brakes and squealed to a stop. There were Tim and Pietro, the truck pulled off the road. And beside it stood a car and horse trailer.

"What is it, Tim?" Ed asked, as his son approached.

"That's what I'd like to know, Dad," the boy said softly. "Pietro insists that this is the place where he and Juan left the highway and went into the hills."

"What does he say about this other car?"

"He claims he knows nothing about it."

They all got out of the jeep, and Pietro came over to join them.

"What about this car, Pietro?" Ed asked. There was a trace of sharpness in his voice.

The Indian shrugged his shoulders.

"This country, she was once the place of many mines," he said. "My people tell about them. Everywhere the mines." He gestured toward the mountains with a wide sweep of his arm. "The *Americanos* they come and run everywhere, looking, looking, looking."

Ed motioned Tim aside with a toss of his head.

"What do you think?" he asked.

"I don't know. I've done everything I could to get some information out of Pietro, but he claims to know nothing. To tell you the truth, Dad, he acts as though this is just a routine trip."

Ed kicked a pebble with his foot.

"I thought we ought to take the girls on up to the mission," he said, "before going into the hills."

"I don't know, Dad," Tim went on. "Do you think we dare take the time? It will mean another day or day and a half. And if those guys who own this car are after our ore, they've already got a head start."

The older man ran his fingers through his graying hair.

"I know what you say is right," he answered slowly, "but I can't feel entirely easy about the girls. I wish we had left them back in Alamos." He sighed deeply.

CHAPTER 8

IN THE HILLS

Sue motioned Felicia away from the others with a slight toss of her head. The Cartright girl waited a moment, until Joan asked Nina Bauer a question. Then she edged away.

"Let's go over and talk to Dad," Sue whispered. "He'll let us go along if we coax him."

"I don't want to interfere," Felicia answered, "and I'm sure that Nina and Joan don't either. He'll decide what's best."

"But the only reason he doesn't want to take us is because he's afraid we might get hurt. He likes to have us around. He's taken me prospecting lots of times." She glanced quickly at her dad and Tim. "Besides, if he takes us all the way to the mission first, he's apt to lose the claim to this other guy. The man has a head start on us already."

Before Felicia could answer, Ed Collins came over to where the two girls were standing.

"What was she doing, Felicia?" he asked, a smile on his lips. "Trying to coax you into helping her wrap me around her finger?"

Felicia colored slightly.

"You don't have to answer that," he went on. "I know my Susan. She's a sorcerer at heart."

"Dad," Sue countered, "you make me sound terrible."

"Now, Kitten, I meant that as a compliment," he told her. "As a matter of fact, I came to inform you that your sorcery has already worked."

Sue stared at him. "You mean we're going along?" she asked.

"I wanted to talk with you and Felicia and the others about it," he said. "I don't think there's any danger. If I did, I'd insist on taking you to the mission, even if I knew that it would cost us the claim."

"I know that we want you to do whatever you think is best," Felicia said.

"I'd much prefer taking you to the mission," Ed answered, "but finding this car here does change the matter considerably. The chances are that our friends who own it are after the same thing we are."

"Oh, Ed!" Felicia exclaimed. "That's terrible!"

"Well," he continued, "they haven't found it yet. At least I don't think they have. And between Pietro and myself, I believe we know these hills as well or better than anyone else who is apt to be prospecting in the area. We've still got a chance, especially if we can leave now without going to the mission."

"Oh, Dad!" Sue cried, kissing him impulsively on the cheek. "You're a dear!"

They got the horses out of the truck, loaded the gear on the pack animals, and started down the trail. It was wide near the highway, and they rode double file.

"This is wonderful," Sue said to Felicia. "I was afraid that Dad wasn't going to let us go along. He's so terribly cautious. He says it comes from spending so many years prospecting in the hills."

For several minutes Felicia did not speak. She stared in awe at the magnificent mountains all about them.

Pietro seemed in no mood to hurry, and Tim chafed with impatience.

"Pietro!" he called out. "Can't we get a move on? We've got a lot of distance to cover!"

"*Sí,*" the Indian retorted blandly. "It is much far to go, and we like for to have our horses last until they get there."

"He's right, Tim," Ed put in. "We'll cover a great deal of ground in a day at this speed."

Felicia and Sue were riding slowly behind the others, drinking in the majestic beauty around them.

"Did Nina tell you what she is going to do at the mission?" Sue asked after a time.

"I think she's going to teach the children of the

other missionaries," Felicia answered. "And, of course, she'll help bring the gospel to the people in the area."

Sue placed her hand on the saddle horn and leaned forward.

"I can see why they would want to teach the people to read," she said, "and why they would try to make them all see the importance of a better diet, good sanitation, and cleanliness. I can see why they'd want to improve their standard of living. Those things are important."

"More important than a soul?" Felicia asked gently.

Sue squirmed uncomfortably.

"Wouldn't it be better to leave them alone with their religion? They're happy and contented just the way they are. Why should we come in with a religion that's made for a different culture and try to force it on them?"

Felicia brushed the perspiration from her face.

"The Bible has the only answer, Sue," she said. "In the book of Acts we're told, *Neither is there salvation in any other; for there is none other name under heaven given among men, whereby we must be saved.*"

Sue turned the verse slowly in her mind.

"But those people are so sincere, Felicia," she continued. "We've talked about this a great deal at home. We've always felt that when it came to religion, it doesn't make any difference what we believe so long as we're sincere about it."

"I think that scheelite ore is up here half a mile,"

Felicia said suddenly. "I firmly believe that it's there. I think we ought to stop and stake out our claim."

Sue stared at her incredulously.

"Suppose we had headed south out of Alamos instead of north," Felicia continued. "We firmly believe that we're going north. How long would it take us to get to the mission?"

"We never would get there," Sue answered, "but I don't see–"

"Let me finish," Felicia went on. "Last night we all believed that it was impossible for anyone to break into the house. We were sure of it. Once those doors and windows were locked, no one could get in. Isn't that the way it was?"

"That's the way it was," Sue said, a bit irritably. "At least we thought that's the way it was, but you know as well as I do what actually happened."

Felicia Cartright nodded.

"That's right," she said. "I know what happened, in spite of the fact that we were very sincere about believing that we were completely safe and that no one could get in."

She paused for a moment or two, allowing her cousin to get the full meaning of her words.

"You can't name a single thing on the face of the earth in which believing something and being sincere about it will make it true. Why should religion be the single exception? A person who puts his trust in something other than the Lord Jesus for salvation, regardless of how sincere he might be, is as far off as a man who is sincerely mistaken about the road he is on. Both are completely lost, and they'll never get where they think they are going. The Bible tells us clearly that we must confess our sin and put our trust in Jesus if we want to be saved and go to heaven. There is no other way, whether we are sincere in believing there is or not."

They rode on for almost half a mile before Sue Collins spoke once more.

"But God is a God of love," she protested. "He loves us so much that He won't let us be lost, regardless of what we do." She spoke defensively.

"He is a God of love," Felicia admitted, "but He also is a God of justice. He provides laws for us to live by and punishment for those who break those laws. When we proved to be too weak to keep them, He loved us so very much that He sent His only Son, Jesus Christ, to die on the cross so that we might be saved."

Sue was breathing heavily.

"That would mean that I'm a sinner," she said, almost under her breath.

"The Bible says *all have sinned and come short of the glory of God.*"

"But I've tried to be as good as I could," Sue continued. "I don't smoke or drink or swear, and I try my best to respect Dad and do what he wants me to. I don't think I'm so bad."

"*There is none righteous,*" Felicia continued quoting. "*No, not one.*"

For a moment or two it looked as though Sue was about to cry. Then she looked up and noticed that the others were some distance ahead of them.

"Come on, Felicia!" she said, changing the subject abruptly. "The others are getting a long way ahead of us."

Although they rode until almost dark and saw evidence of the other prospectors frequently, they did not see them.

"They must have gotten quite a head start on us, Dad," Tim said.

Ed Collins nodded in agreement.

"There are two of them. We know that much," he said. "And they're traveling light. They've only got one pack animal."

"If we had only started yesterday," Tim said. "Those guys have quite a lead on us, Dad. It's got me concerned."

"But we've got Pietro with us," Ed answered. "That will make quite a difference. And I've done a lot of prospecting in this part of the country. That ought to give us a little more of an advantage. I haven't given up by a long way."

"Neither have I," the boy said doubtfully. "But I'll sure feel a lot better when we get the claim staked out and recorded."

They stopped for the night soon, and Felicia and

Nina cooked supper while Joan and Sue helped with the sleeping bags.

"What's the matter between you and Sue?" the Bailey girl whispered to Felicia when she had the opportunity.

"Why?"

"She acts as though she's avoiding you," Joan answered.

"We had a talk about spiritual things this afternoon," Felicia answered. "I think it disturbed her a little."

"I'll be praying for her," Joan said.

Two more days passed slowly in the scorching sun and wind. Pietro kept the pace slow and deliberate, but they did move forward with a sureness that seemed to indicate he knew exactly where he was leading them. Nevertheless, Tim was still uneasy.

"Are we on the right trail, Dad?" he asked.

"Pietro!" Ed called out.

The Indian stopped and turned his mount, a strange, inscrutable look on his face.

"Are we on the right trail?" the prospector asked him. His voice was kind but firm.

"What does the map say?" Pietro asked.

"It says we're right," Ed agreed, "but I thought perhaps you would remember something about the country that would indicate whether we were right or not."

"Follow the map," Pietro repeated, shrugging his

shoulders. "Soon we be there. It take long time for to go so far. Much long."

They rode down into the valley, across the river, and over against the highest ridge of mountains that rimmed the Yaqui Valley. Pietro rode ahead, stolidly, nodding in the saddle.

"Dad," Tim said once more, "I'm getting more uneasy about this all the time. I know what the map says, but you and I studied it for two hours the other night. I know we ought to be up on that ridge."

"I've been thinking the same thing," Ed agreed. "As I recall the map, we were to follow the ridge most of the way. But we were awfully excited. We could have been mistaken."

"I suppose so," Tim answered. But his voice revealed plainly that he was unconvinced.

Felicia, who was riding beside Joan just behind them that afternoon, started slightly. She had seen the map, too, and she was sure they were right.

"Now if we had come out here without Pietro or the map," she thought silently, "I'd have figured we should have turned off at the trail back there and gone along that ridge."

Her gaze traveled to the row of hills that lay along the edge of the valley. As she did so, she caught a glimpse of a lone figure standing out against the horizon.

"Look up there!" she cried sharply.

The little group stopped.

"There's our friend!" Tim exclaimed.

Then there were two of them.

Ed Collins did not speak, but he took his high-powered field glasses from their case and began to study the ridge intently.

"That's Juan! I'd recognize that yellow shirt of his anywhere!"

As he spoke, Pietro turned his horse and faced them.

"What is this, Pietro?" Ed Collins demanded. This time there was steel in his voice.

CHAPTER 9

"STAY WHERE YOU ARE!"

There was a faint stir in the rocks behind them, the sound of cautious footsteps. Felicia heard it, she remembered afterward, but for the moment the tense drama that was unfolding before her seemed to hypnotize her.

"Pietro!" Ed Collins exclaimed hotly. "You've got some tall talking to do, pronto. What's Juan doing up there? Why did he come here with another prospector?"

"But *señor,*" the Indian answered placidly, "Juan, he no have to ask Pietro if he go into the hills."

Ed Collins heard the sound once more and whirled around.

At the same instant, Joan Bailey screamed. Ed cried out involuntarily. They were looking into the ugly, black barrel of a heavy rifle.

"Put your hands in the air," the man with the gun grated. "High!"

"Spanner!" Ed exclaimed.

"Stay where you are!" the voice ordered.

There was fright in it. A strange, desperate sort of fright, Felicia and the others realized. The sort of fright that could cause him to pull the trigger if someone coughed.

"You're the man in the hotel!" Felicia exclaimed.

Spanner laughed humorlessly. "Strange how many interesting things you can pick up in a hotel lobby," he continued. "We've been watching you, Collins, ever since you got that mineral light and got so secretive, but I sure didn't figure on getting the information from the hotel lobby."

"I might have known it would be you," the prospector said evenly.

"Keep those hands up!" The big gun wavered in Martin Spanner's bony fingers. His features were small, and the harsh, subtropical sun had burned him to a deep mahogany. A life of drinking and waste had etched deep wrinkles around his mouth and the corners of his blood-shot eyes.

"You can't get away with this, you know," Ed warned him.

Felicia shifted uneasily in the saddle and glanced back at Sue and Nina.

"You, back there!" Spanner exclaimed. "Don't try anything! I've got this gun on you! Remember that!"

"What do you plan to do with us?" Sue asked, her voice tremoring.

"He isn't going to hurt us, Sue," Ed answered. "Just keep calm and do as he says."

Spanner laughed nervously.

"That's the best advice you've ever given anyone. See that you follow it yourself." He cast a quick look toward the Indian guide. "Get over there, Pietro," he said. "You did a good job of leading them out here. A fine job. But I'll take over now."

Felicia tensed in the saddle. She was the closest to the man with the gun. If he took his eyes off her for an instant, she could jab her horse in the ribs and knock the man down before he could pull the trigger. They could all ride into the hills before he got to his feet again. For an instant, she considered the possibility.

But what of Pietro? Was he armed? What would he do in a situation like that?

"You're making a mistake, Spanner," Ed Collins said. "You can't get away with a thing like this, and you know it."

The American with the gun eyed him warily.

"You," he growled, motioning to Tim, "get off that horse and tie up the old man."

Tim hesitated.

"Hurry up! And don't try any funny stuff!"

"You'd better do as he says, Tim," his dad said quietly.

"Now you're talking sense, Collins," Spanner said. He grinned evilly. "Keep that up and everything will be all right. All right."

Tim gritted his teeth and did as he was told. When he had his dad's hands tied securely above the saddle horn and a foot to each stirrup, Spanner made him do the same to the girls.

"I'm sorry about this, Joan," Tim said under his breath as he tied her hands. "I'll try to tie them so they won't hurt too much."

"I'm not exactly used to riding this way," Joan said, "but we'll be all right. Don't worry about us."

"I should have let Dad take you girls on to the mission the way he wanted to."

"This isn't your fault," Joan answered. "And we were all anxious to come."

Tim glanced up.

"If you believe so much in that praying of yours, you'd better be doing a lot of it. This guy, Spanner, is dangerous. He's scared to death right now. The least little thing might cause him to fire."

"You two!" the man with the gun said sharply. "Cut that talk!" He turned to Pietro. "Better check those ropes, Pietro," he ordered.

A strange, almost helpless look came into the Indian's eyes as he jerked on the ropes that bound Ed's hands.

"I didn't think you'd do this to me," Ed Collins said softly. "I always thought I could trust you, Pietro."

"Shut up!" Spanner demanded coldly.

He ordered Tim to mount his horse and directed Pietro to tie him.

"What are you going to do to us?" Sue Collins asked. Her voice was taut and trembling.

"Suppose you let me worry about that," Spanner reported. "Just do as you're told, and everything will be all right."

"Everything's going to be all right, Sue," Felicia told the frightened girl gently.

Sue's eyes sought hers.

"H-h-h-how can you be so calm?" she asked. There was a strange note in her voice.

Spanner got a horse from behind the rocks and started the little party down the trail. He made them ride single file and ordered them not to talk.

Once they reached the muddy Yaqui River, the prospector allowed them to dismount and, freeing Joan, ordered her to cook supper.

"For everybody?" Joan asked, eyeing him.

He nodded.

"You're making a mistake," she said. "I'm not much of a cook."

"Then you can learn."

"Have you got a good cookbook?" she asked. "I never cook without a cookbook."

Spanner's face twisted with anger.

"Let me help her," Felicia said.

"What's the matter, Spanner?" Tim asked, his voice

edged with steel. "There are two of you, and at least you have a gun. Are you afraid that two unarmed girls will be able to take it away from you?"

The little man flushed, but he nodded to Pietro. "Let her loose. But mind you, girl, no funny stuff."

"You're a life saver, Felicia," Joan said. "And with me cooking, I don't mean *my* life."

The tall, lanky Indian shuffled to the other side of the fire where he squatted and watched them. Spanner sat a dozen or so paces away, leaning up against a rock. The rifle was across his lap.

Ed leaned back until his lips were almost in his son's ears.

"We've got to do something, Tim," he whispered.

"But what can we do?"

Pietro got to his feet and moved toward the fire to shove another twisted branch into it.

"Go ahead and talk," Spanner said to Ed. He laughed shortly. "You're both tied up. There's nothing you can do until after we get the claim staked and filed on. By then, it'll be too late!"

When they had finished eating, Pietro tied Joan and Felicia once more.

"We are praying for you, Pietro," Felicia told the Indian softly.

He looked up at her, his dark eyes narrowing.

"For me, *señorita?*" he asked. There was a new and different tone in his voice. "Why you pray for me?"

"Because you need Jesus Christ as your Savior,"

she said, "just as we all need Him. I'll pray that God will speak to your heart until you confess your sin and trust Him as your Savior."

He shook his head in bewilderment.

"I'll be praying for you too," Nina added.

"No one ever pray for Pietro before," he said. "No one ever do that before."

He walked thoughtfully away.

"Now I can understand that," Sue whispered from her sleeping bag on the other side of Felicia. "To me salvation is for men like that."

"The Bible says that salvation is for all of us," Felicia reminded her.

Sue looked at her appealingly for a moment, then turned on her side. Felicia prayed in silence for her and Pietro. When she finished and looked toward Joan, she saw that her friend was doing the same.

Martin Spanner came up noisily just then, dragging a long, twisted limb he had found along the riverbank.

"Come on, Pietro," he called. "Cut this for firewood. I'll go back for another one."

While they were so occupied, Tim turned to his dad. "I just thought of something, Dad," he whispered. "I think I know why they put that map in the car after they stole it."

"I think they wanted to be sure that we'd take Pietro along so he would lead us into this trap," Ed answered.

The girls, who were lying in their sleeping bags nearby, could just hear them.

"I'm afraid this is all my fault," the missionary said. "This man, Spanner, wouldn't have found out anything if I hadn't been in the hotel."

"That's hard to say," Ed answered. "Pietro could have gotten hold of him. Somebody else could have given him a tip. You didn't do it purposely, at any rate." He smiled reassuringly at her. "So don't worry about it, Nina."

"Dad," Tim broke in, "listen to me. They wanted us to take Pietro all right, but they also wanted to make sure we wouldn't get ideas and start ordering him in some other direction. So they changed those marks Pietro made on the map."

Ed thought about that for a moment or two.

"That could have happened," he said. "In fact, it sounds logical. Those three X marks were supposed to mark the three places where Pietro and Juan thought they might have picked up those scheelite-bearing rocks."

"So, while we stumble along down here, Juan and another prospector are headed straight for the places where they got the ore."

"That's it, Tim," his dad exclaimed under his breath. "That's the answer."

"But why would they come and capture us this way?" Tim insisted.

"Maybe this is just a little more insurance," Ed

went on. "You know the stakes are big in this deal, and they want to be sure that nothing happens to get it away from them."

Spanner and Pietro came back to the fire and began to roll out their blankets. The men stopped talking.

For an hour or more, Felicia and Joan lay in the darkness looking around silently. The ropes on their hands and feet hurt terribly, and they found it difficult to get to sleep.

"If there were only something we could do," Felicia whispered to her friend.

"I'd be satisfied right now if I could get to sleep," Joan answered. "I'm so tired I can scarcely keep my eyes open, but I can't get comfortable."

"I haven't been asleep either," Nina said. "I've been thinking about those men and praying for them and for us."

Sue rolled over on her side to face them.

"I can't understand you girls," she said. "I can't understand you at all. Here we are in danger of our lives and you're praying for the guys who have captured us."

"Jesus directs us to always pray for our enemies," Nina told her. "Besides, Pietro and Spanner wouldn't be that way if they knew Jesus as their Savior."

Sue sighed deeply, wearily, and closed her eyes.

After a time, the girls went to sleep. It was an hour or two later that Felicia stirred and awakened. For a moment she lay there looking around. The fire had gone out. There was no sound except the muffled gurgling of the water in the darkness and the slow, rhythmical breathing of the others. She raised on one elbow.

There were Ed and Tim and the girls, but – her throat choked suddenly. Spanner and Pietro were gone!

"Ed!" she shouted. "Ed! They're gone!" Instantly everyone was awake.

"What is it, Felicia?" her cousin demanded. "What's the matter?"

"It–it's Pietro and Spanner," she said. "They're both gone!"

"Their blankets are gone too!" Ed exclaimed. It was Tim who looked toward the place where the horses had been grazing. In the faint moonlight, he could make out the little stretch of grass.

"And so are our horses!" he said numbly. "Pietro and Spanner took our horses too!"

CHAPTER 10

STRANDED

Time stood still in the silence that enveloped the tense little group. Even the wind lowered its whisper across the valley, and the gurgling of the river was muted and faint, a tremulous obligato in the night by an uncertain soloist.

Felicia looked around. In the moonlight, she could see the other members of the little party plainly. They were wide-eyed and staring, their faces reflecting the danger of this new situation.

"M-maybe the horses wandered off," Sue ventured lamely. "Maybe if we get free, we'll find them feeding along the river."

Her dad answered, "I'm afraid not, Kitten. If it had been Juan or Spanner who picketed those horses, I'd agree with you. They're both careless. But not Pietro. He has worked for me for three years, and I've never known an animal he had tied to break loose."

A weak little moan escaped Sue's lips.

"We're stranded," she said numbly. "They've gone and left us afoot and without food or water." She spoke softly and with a certain control, but Felicia caught a note of hysteria creeping in.

She turned to her.

"Sue," she said gently, "we have God to turn to."

Sue moistened her lips but did not speak.

"Maybe those horses are close by," Tim said. "I can't imagine Pietro leaving us out here without *any* means of getting back. Maybe he just took the horses a few miles away and tied them where we could find them."

Gritting his teeth, he struggled to get to his feet, but the rope bit savagely into his ankles. Suppressing a quick, involuntary groan, he sank back to the ground.

Ed Collins was working vigorously, trying to free his hands.

"What are we going to do?" Joan asked. There was a trace of fear in her voice but no wild, unreasoning desperation.

"Why don't we pray now?" Nina Bauer asked quietly. "God tells us that Christians should turn to Him in time of trouble."

"But Felicia said that we weren't Christians!" Sue blurted.

Fire leaped, for the first time, to Ed Collins' eyes.

"What was that?" he demanded coldly. He spoke

to his daughter, but his gaze was boring deep into Felicia's eyes.

"No," Felicia answered. She knew that her cheeks were tinged with color. "I didn't say that you weren't Christians, Sue."

"But you said that about sin and–" her voice trailed away.

"I only quoted the Bible to you," the girl continued. "Verses which say that each person is lost. *All we like sheep have gone astray; we have turned every one to his own way; and the Lord has laid on him the iniquity of us all.* And, *the wages of sin is death, but the gift of God is eternal life through Jesus Christ, our Lord.*"

There was a short silence.

"That's the same thing," Ed retorted. He was angry, violently angry, although his voice did not raise. "I don't like having anyone tell Sue she isn't a Christian. She's a good girl. A fine girl."

"It's not for me or any other person to say who's a Christian," Felicia continued, "and who isn't. Only God knows the condition of a heart. And only the condition of the heart can save. The Bible tells us that we can't possibly be good enough to earn salvation."

"That's right," Nina added softly. "And, Mr. Collins, we may not like what the Bible says. We may think we're so good that we don't need a Savior, and reading the Bible where God says differently may hurt us terribly. But that doesn't change the situation. The Bible is still God's Word. There is still only one way to be saved, and that is for a person to confess his sin and put his trust in Christ to save. That's why He died on the cross."

The silence was deafening.

"If you're going to pray," Ed retorted, at last, hoarsely, "let's get on with it."

They all bowed their heads, and Nina, Joan, and Felicia prayed in turn for safety and wisdom.

"And, God," Felicia continued, "speak to our hearts through Your Spirit. Convict us of sin and our need for salvation."

When she finished, Ed glared at her. "You didn't have to pray that way," he retorted.

"Dad," Tim broke in, "I think the rope on my hands is getting a little loose. Do you suppose you could do anything with it?"

"Back over here, and I'll see."

Ed tried to use his hands to loosen the knot that tied his son, but he could not. Pietro had drawn the rope tightly.

"Hold up your hands a little higher," he said. "I'll do what I can with my teeth."

"You can't untie them that way."

Nevertheless, Tim raised his arms until his dad could bend over to find the knot with his teeth. Ed Collins explored the knot, speculatively, with the tip of his tongue. The rope was hard twist. It rasped against his tongue as he followed the bends in the knot.

He looked up for an instant. "I've found the place

to work on, Tim," he said. "And I'm going to have to jerk. It might hurt."

"Go ahead. That rope hasn't been exactly comfortable the way it is."

The older man bit savagely into the hard rope and pulled with all the strength he could gather. His teeth ached. His whole being throbbed with pain.

Tim groaned. "Hey, Dad, take it easy! That's me in there!"

Ed only pulled harder.

At first, the rope was immovable. He jerked on it again and again.

"I think it's coming!" he cried at last.

It did seem to have yielded slightly. Not much. Only a fraction of a fraction of an inch.

Felicia and Joan and the missionary were praying silently.

In two or three minutes, Ed had the first loop of the knot free. A tremor ran through his body. In a moment, Tim cried out exultantly.

"You did it, Dad! You did it!"

"Thank God!" Felicia said prayerfully.

Tim rubbed his wrists painfully, before untying his dad's hands and feet. In two or three minutes, they were all free.

"Boy, that feels good!" Tim said over and over again. "I didn't know whether we'd ever get free or not."

Sue was looking around fearfully.

"Where do you suppose Pietro and that awful Mr. Spanner went?" she asked.

"They're a long way from here by this time, Kitten," her dad said. "They've gone up on the ridge where we saw Juan and his companion late yesterday afternoon. Up where we ought to be."

"What are we going to do," she asked.

"We could follow them," Tim said. "They haven't got too much of a lead on us."

"On foot?" his dad asked. "We wouldn't be able to get very far, I'm afraid. You want to remember that I've got this game leg. I'm not able to do much walking of any kind."

Felicia stiffened. Up until that moment, getting free seemed to solve every problem. Now what were they going to do? What could they do?

"Is there anyone who lives around here, Dad?" Tim asked. "Anyone who would loan or sell us horses? Or at least help us get back to our car and truck?"

"That's just what I was thinking. Get the flashlight, Tim, and let's take a look at that map again."

They unfolded the map and began to study it carefully.

"There's a ranch here," Ed said after a time. "I've stopped there and bought supplies a time or two."

Tim glanced at the map scale and did a quick calculation. "That's quite a ways, Dad," he said. "It would take me all day and maybe half of the night to make it. But I believe it's best, don't you?"

Ed nodded.

"It's the only thing I can think of. This leg of mine wouldn't last a mile on the trail, and I don't know whether the girls could make it that far or not. It's doubtful in this heat."

Ed got another map from his saddle bag and carefully marked Tim's route.

"Now I know this rancher," he said. "Tell him who you are, and he'll fix us up. We'll be waiting for you here."

Tim made sure that he understood the map and started away at a brisk pace.

"Goodbye, Tim!" Felicia said to him. "We'll be praying for you."

He grinned at her. "I'm sure going to need it."

He waved to them and disappeared into the shadows.

Sue Collins turned to her father. "Do–do you think he'll be able to get help?" she asked uncertainly.

"Of course, he will, Kitten. Now I think we'd all better go back to bed and get some sleep."

"W-w-what if Spanner and Pietro come back?" Joan asked. "I sure don't want to take a chance on having them catch us again."

"They won't be coming back," Ed told her reassuringly. "They've got business up on that ridge, and they're going to get there just as fast as they can."

"I–I hope you're right," Sue replied uncertainly.

CHAPTER II

HARD RIDING AHEAD

Morning came at last, gray and shadowless, but with a blazing arc of fire on the horizon to give hint of another scorching day. The girls and Ed Collins got up stiffly and looked around. Nobody said very much.

"Fortunately, they didn't take our food," Felicia said.

"That proves that they're not so bad at heart," Nina Bauer put in. "They could have taken everything and left us to starve."

"They left us on foot," Sue countered angrily. "That was bad enough!"

"I'll start the fire," Ed put in, "if you girls want to start breakfast. I'm about starved."

When they had finished eating, Joan glanced about. "You know," she said, "I always thought there were a lot of Indians living in these mountains. Especially down along the rivers."

"There are," Ed said. "There are quite a few small farms and ranches through here."

"It's too bad there weren't any closer," she went on. "We could probably have gotten horses from them."

Ed was interested immediately.

"I think you've got something, Joan," he said, "that neither Tim nor I thought of. These small ranches aren't listed on the maps we're using. Only the bigger spreads are marked."

"Then there is a chance that there's a small ranch nearby?"

"A very good chance," Ed replied excitedly. "Especially down along the river. This area is quite dry, so the ranchers all have to have access to a creek or a river."

"Maybe Tim will run across one before he gets to where he's going," Felicia put in. "That would save a great deal of time."

"Only he's cutting across country," Ed said. "I don't think he'll find anything in the territory he'll be going through until he reaches the ranch I marked."

The girls looked at one another.

"We could go," Felicia ventured.

"I don't know," her cousin said. "It's going to be another scorching day, and you aren't used to the sort of heat we have around here."

"But it's early," Nina said. "We could follow the river. That way we wouldn't get lost. And if we get too tired, we could stop and rest or even turn back."

Ed hesitated.

"It's the only thing we can do, Ed," Felicia said. "It will be two days before Tim gets back. We might be a mile from a ranch."

"I don't like the idea much," he said after a time, "but I'll have to agree with you. I don't have a better plan."

"We'd better leave now." Felicia turned back to the other girls. "There's no need in all of us going," she said. "Why don't you and Joan stay here with your dad, Sue? Nina and I will go."

"You stay here," Joan said, "and we'll go."

Felicia shook her head. "If we don't find anything upstream, you can go downstream tonight or in the morning."

The two girls started up the sluggish, silt-laden river. Although it was early morning, there were no clouds in the sky, and the sun was already blasting the hills with savage intensity.

"We're going to have to take it easy," Nina said, wiping the grimy perspiration from her face. "In this heat, we could get sunstroke easily."

"I thought Sue and Joan looked as though the heat were affecting them," Felicia said, "as though they didn't have strength enough to walk a half mile. That's why I suggested that we go."

Nina laughed easily.

"You don't have to apologize," she said. "I wouldn't miss it for anything."

They kept to the shade of the trees along the river as much as possible.

"I've been concerned about Sue," Nina said after a time. "I've tried to talk with her about the things of Christ, but she cut me off short. For a while, I was afraid I had made her angry."

"Joan and I have been talking with her too. Somehow, she has the idea that she's living a good enough life, so she won't need a Savior."

Nina shook her head sorrowfully.

"And the pitiful thing is," she said, "Sue does live a good life by human standards. I suppose a person of the world would say that she lives an almost perfect life. It's so hard to make people like that see that they need a Savior."

Felicia would have answered, but they came around a bend in the river, and she saw something that caused her to stop suddenly.

"What's the matter?" Nina asked curiously.

"Look over there," she said. "We're not far from a farm or ranch or something."

She pointed to the barbed-wire fence that blocked their path.

"Felicia!" Nina squealed with delight. "God has answered our prayers. We've found someone!"

"Now to see if we can get horses from them," the Cartright girl said. "I wish Ed were here. What do we do if the person doesn't speak English?"

The missionary smiled. "Now, Felicia," she said,

"you don't think that God would lead us to a ranch and people we couldn't talk to, do you?"

They hurried on. Felicia's heart was beating faster, and her breath was coming in thin, quick jerks.

At last they reached the ranch house. It was almost as decrepit as its wizened, brown-skinned owners. The man and woman both came out in the yard and eyed Nina and Felicia critically.

"Do you have any saddle horses?" Felicia asked, pronouncing the words slowly. "Any saddle horses?"

They wrinkled their faces. "Horses?" the man echoed just as the girls were despairing of making him understand. "*Sí,* we have horses."

They explained how many they wanted and why they wanted them.

The old man shook his head. "One horse you could buy," he said. "Two horse maybe we could sell you, but five horses?" He gestured expressively. "So many horses we could not spare."

Felicia and Nina stared at one another helplessly.

"The mission is not far from here," Nina said. "We could leave them there for you. Or we could have one of the men from the mission bring them back to you."

"The mission?" he echoed. "You belong with the mission?"

"I'm going there to work," Nina told him.

His wrinkled, old face softened. He spoke to his wife in a torrent of Spanish.

A broad smile lit her face.

"From the mission?" she echoed. "Of course, we have horses for you. And saddles too."

"We're willing to pay you," Felicia told them.

"Pay us?" His voice crescendoed indignantly. "You talk of pay to us? It was the people at the mission who come and talk with us about the Lord Jesus. It is because of them that we are Christians now. No, you can no pay us for the horses."

The old man hobbled out to the barn, caught five horses, and saddled them.

Nina and Felicia both thanked them. They had a word of prayer together, and the girls rode off, heading back in the direction from where they had come.

"Weren't they wonderful people?" Felicia asked.

"Yes," Nina said. "Have you ever noticed how the gospel changes people? You'd have thought we were friends or some close relatives the way they treated us, and we'd never seen them before."

Ed Collins and the girls were sitting around the campfire eating dinner when Felicia and Nina rode up.

"You got them!" Sue cried, running to meet them. "You got horses for us!"

"Sure," Felicia said. "That's what we went after."

"You make it sound as easy as going to the store for a can of pork and beans."

"It was, almost."

"What did you have to pay for them?" Ed asked. "Did I give you enough money?"

"More than enough," Felicia told him, handing him his money belt. "They wouldn't take a cent."

He stared at her.

"What did you say?" he exclaimed.

"They wouldn't take anything for the use of the horses," she repeated.

"When they found out that I was associated with the mission they told us they still wouldn't sell them," Nina went on, "but they would let us use them."

Sue's face lit up. "I suppose they had gotten medicine at the dispensary," she said. "I've heard about those things happening. Dad was telling how grateful some of the people in these out-of-the-way places are for medical help."

"It wasn't medical help they got," Nina countered. "They were grateful because of spiritual help. Because the missionaries had presented Jesus Christ to them and they confessed their sins and put their trust in the Lord Jesus."

A peculiar look came to Sue's face; a hurt, bewildered look that gave a quick peek to the very depths of her heart.

Ed came over and joined them.

"What do you think we ought to do?" he asked. "Follow Tim or try to follow Pietro and Spanner?"

"If we don't follow Tim," Sue asked, "how will he ever find us, Dad?"

"We can leave word for him here," Ed said. "We can put a note in that fruit jar and seal it. It might make the difference between finding the claim first or failing."

"If you think Tim will be all right," Sue said.

"He can take care of himself."

"But do you think we'll be able to follow Pietro and his friend?" Joan asked. "Won't they try to hide their trail?"

"Why should they?" Ed asked. "They don't know that we have horses. They think we'll get loose, all right, and they figure that eventually we'll make it to some rancher's place, but they don't figure on seeing us again until after they find the ore and get the claim staked out and filed on."

"But do we want to follow those two men?" Felicia asked. "Didn't you say they had changed the map?"

"I don't get what you're driving at, Felicia," Ed told her.

"Do you suppose we can see the places where they made the erasures?" she asked. "We might still be able to find where the spots are. Then, all we'd have to do is figure out which ones those guys have already visited and go to the next one."

Ed did not answer her. Instead, he brought out the map and, spreading it before them on the parched ground, began to study it intently.

"Doesn't that look like an erasure mark?" Felicia asked, pointing to a faint smudge with her finger.

"And there's another," he said. "Whoever changed this map must have done it in a big hurry. I don't see why we didn't notice that before." His eyes and the tone of his voice betrayed his excitement. "Those marks they erased must have indicated the places where they picked up ore on that trip. The new marks are the places they wanted us to think they located the ore."

"Then all we've got to do is pick the right one," Felicia said. By this time, all the girls were crowding around.

"Now we saw Juan over here, almost in line with that second mark. That happened the night Spanner jumped us," Ed said. "It could explain why he did it. He could have been trailing us, and when we started in the direction of Juan and the guy who was with him, Spanner could have figured he had to do something. So he jumped us to keep us from leaving Pietro and following Juan."

"Remember how high he insisted on building the fire that night, Dad," Sue said. "And how he went off by himself and looked toward the ridge for so long."

"He was probably signaling to Juan and waiting for Juan to signal back," Joan said. "It would have had to be something like that, or Spanner and Pietro wouldn't have run off and left us."

Ed studied the map once more.

"That's why I figure they didn't find the scheelite at either of the first two locations. If Juan had done so, he would have scooted back to Alamos to register the claim. There wouldn't have been any point in Spanner and Pietro running off and leaving us. The only explanation is that the scheelite is here, at number three."

Ed got to his feet abruptly.

"Come on," he said. "We've got some hard riding to do!"

CHAPTER 12

A DARK TRAIL

They mounted and forded the shallow, muddy river.

"You know," Sue said to Felicia, "I was so tired a little while ago that I didn't think I'd ever be able to move again. Now I feel as fresh as though I just got up."

The Cartright girl smiled. The same excitement gripped her too.

"Do you think we can find the scheelite?" Sue went on.

"Your dad seems to think we can," Felicia answered.

"It scarcely seems real to me," Sue went on. "Just think, Felicia! We might all be rich!"

Felicia turned in the saddle and looked at her.

"That doesn't concern me at all," she said. "The important thing in this world is following Christ and doing His will."

Sue reined in, and, for an instant, she faced Felicia in silence.

"I don't know what's the matter with me," she said at last. Her voice was as serious as the look in her eyes. "Ever since you started talking about things like that, I haven't been able to think of much else. I've even been waking up in the middle of the night."

"That's the Holy Spirit talking to you, Sue," Felicia told her. "He is urging you to accept Christ as your Savior."

"I used to feel that I was so good I didn't need a Savior," Sue went on. "But now I'm not so sure. Last night I laid awake for a long while thinking about it. I–I'm beginning to see what you girls have been telling me."

Felicia prayed silently.

"The whole thing is that we try to classify sin," she said. "We try to say that this is a very wicked thing and that isn't so bad. So, if I only do the things people think aren't so bad, I'm all right. But the Bible tells us that God doesn't do that. Sin is sin, and the wages of sin is death."

Sue's face was chalk-white, and her lips were trembling.

"I've always thought I was a Christian," she went on. "I've never doubted that there is a God or that Jesus came or anything like that. And I have tried to be good."

"But, Sue," Felicia told her insistently, "until you

have met the conditions God has laid down, until you have confessed your sin and put your trust in Jesus Christ, that doesn't do you any good. You can believe all about Christ, but you've got to put your trust in Him."

The others had gone on a quarter of a mile or so ahead of them, but that made no difference to either Sue or Felicia. Neither of them had noticed it.

"I want to be a Christian, Felicia," Sue said at last. "Ever since you and Joan came, I've wanted to be like you."

Without dismounting, they bowed their heads and prayed.

When they finished, Sue looked up. A faint smile played on her lips, and her eyes were luminous.

"I don't know why I've waited so long," she said. "I've known, almost from that first night, that I was going to do this sooner or later."

They urged their mounts to a gallop and hurried to catch the others.

The afternoon wore on as the little group rode. The sun had completed its blazing arc and settled to rest behind the mountains. The shadows grew long and spread until they blended together in the dull gray of twilight. The coming of the night was a subtle thing. It stole in around the edges of the horizon, creeping across rocks and down into the valleys.

The change was so slight they scarcely noticed it. Distance faded first. Trees and rocks merged together into a thousand unfamiliar shapes. The trail all but disappeared. Almost instinctively, the group rode closer together until their horses brushed shoulder against shoulder, nose against flank.

"I wonder where Tim is," Sue ventured when no one had spoken for a mile or two. "Do you suppose he's gotten to the ranch by this time?"

"He ought to be getting close," her father replied.

"Where are we going to camp?" Joan asked.

Ed glanced back at her. "Are you too tired to go on?" he asked.

"No," she answered, "but we–we aren't going to ride in these mountains after dark, are we?" she asked. Shivers danced up and down her spine.

"It's the only time our mineral light will work," he answered.

"Didn't they steal it?" Sue broke in. "Wasn't that in your saddle bag?"

He shook his head. "I put it there but moved it to my bedroll just before we left. I'd had one stolen, and I didn't want to lose another one."

"We can keep riding," Nina said, "if you think we should."

Felicia and the others nodded. "We surely don't want to cause you any trouble now," she said. "This is the last chance you'll have of getting that claim."

"If you girls are too tired, we'll stop," Ed said, "but I think we ought to see if we can find the ore tonight. If we do locate it, we've got to get the claim staked out so we can get back to Alamos and file on it before they get there."

The girls nodded understandingly.

While they talked, they rode on slowly to the top of a little rise on the mountain trail. Felicia, who was riding with Sue at the rear, reined in.

"Ed," she whispered tensely, "look down there!"

"Where?" he demanded. He pulled up his mount abruptly. "What do you see?"

"Isn't that a campfire?" she asked.

In a moment or two he saw it.

"It is!" he cried under his breath. "That must be Spanner!"

If it had not been for the darkness, she would not have seen the tiny fire in the little clearing below them. It was small and almost smokeless, as only those who have spent long years outdoors know how to build a fire.

"Why do you suppose they camped there?" Nina asked.

"That's just what I've been wondering," Ed answered. "According to the way we read the map this afternoon, we aren't too far from the place where Pietro and Juan picked up that ore."

"You don't suppose they left that half-erased mark on the map just to fool us?" Joan asked. "Do you think it really was carelessness, or did they do it so we'd still be off the trail, even if we managed to get free and tried to find the ore?"

Ed thought for a moment. "That could be," he said, "but somehow it doesn't sound like any of them."

Felicia stared down at the little fire. "You know," she said, "we could slip down there close enough to hear what they're talking about. We could find out why they camped there. They might even talk about the map."

"No," Ed replied quickly, "we couldn't do it."

"But why?" Felicia asked. "There are plenty of trees around here. There wouldn't be any danger."

"This game leg of mine wouldn't let me go, and I couldn't let you girls do it."

"But we won't get into trouble, will we, Joan?" Felicia said.

"No," Joan answered, her voice quavering a little. "No, we won't get into trouble, I–I hope."

Ed Collins was silent for a moment. "If only Tim were here," he said.

"We could be a lot quieter than he could," Felicia went on. "Honestly, Ed, if I thought we'd get into any trouble, I wouldn't even suggest it."

He turned the matter over in his mind.

"You'll promise me that you won't take any chances?"

"Of course."

"You won't have to worry about that," Joan assured him. "One little noise and I'll be back over the mountain like a scared rabbit."

"We've got to find out why they're camping where they are."

"Come on, Joan," Felicia said. "We'll be back in a few minutes, Ed."

The two girls tied their horses to a clump of brush and began to descend quietly down the steep, rocky mountain slope toward the fire.

"I don't know why I let you talk me into things like this," Joan whispered. "Every time I vow that it won't happen again."

"S-s-shh," Felicia cautioned. "They might hear us."

There was a tightness in her throat. Perspiration appeared on her forehead, and she felt her arms gooseflesh, although the night was warm.

It seemed to take hours for them to reach the boulders. They were inching forward now, feeling first with one foot and then the other, for loose stones that might hurtle down the steep hillside. At last, they crept behind a huge granite boulder.

"Can you see them?" Felicia whispered to her companion.

"How can I see them? I haven't even looked."

Felicia raised her head cautiously until she could see the very tip of the little fire, licking its yellow wands skyward.

"Joan!" she whispered breathlessly. "It's them. Spanner and Pietro."

The two men were sitting before the fire.

"I don't know why you had to miss that mineral

light!" Spanner complained irritably. "Now Juan and Denton have to ride all the way back where we left Collins to get it."

"But I tell you, he put it in the saddle bags," Pietro exclaimed. "That's where he always carry it."

"That isn't where he carried it this time."

"If you hadn't dropped the one we stole, we wouldn't have to wait," Pietro reminded him.

"Shut up!" Spanner growled. "Are you sure that Ed even had another mineral light?"

"I see it," the Indian said, his voice rising. "With my own eyes, I see them turn out the lights and see the fire dancing on the rocks. It was a mineral light."

"I should have checked that saddle bag. I shouldn't have taken your word that you knew where it was."

"Juan will be back in two hours," Pietro said. "Then we can go over to where we pick up the ore."

Joan touched Felicia on the arm and motioned back toward the trail above them. Both girls paused a moment, then inched backward cautiously.

In a few minutes, they were back up the mountain to the place where the others were waiting for them.

"You're back," Sue exclaimed. "We've been praying for you."

"Did you find out anything?" Ed asked.

Hurriedly the girls told what they had heard.

"That means we'll have to hurry," Ed replied. "Juan and Denton would travel faster than we would, and we don't know when they left to go back. They could be along any time."

"It sounds as though they're expecting them right away," Joan answered.

"Let's get on the move," Felicia's cousin directed.

They rode on for half a mile or so in tense silence.

"How much farther is it?" Sue asked after another twenty or thirty minutes.

"We can't be far," Ed said. "I checked the map while the girls were spying on Pietro and Spanner." He got it out again and held it across his horse's neck with one hand while he studied it in the beam of his flashlight. "We ought to be right about here. That means we're getting very, very close."

"Do you think we can find the place in the dark?" Nina asked doubtfully.

The moon had come up, softening the darkness a little, but they still could see only a few yards ahead.

"This is the crossroad," Ed said at last. "We turn here and go down to the mountain stream."

"But how will we locate it exactly after we get to the place?" Sue asked. "There's an awful lot of territory, and that X on the map wouldn't be in exactly the right place."

"If that scheelite deposit is as big as I think it is," Ed answered, "all we'll have to do is to get in the general area. The mineral light will do the rest."

They rode on until they came to the creek. Ed reined up. Sue stopped her horse beside his.

"This must be it," he said, his voice catching a little. He dismounted and got out the mineral light. "Now, we'll see what we've got here."

He moved carefully, shining the black light across the rocky ground ahead of him while the girls watched in silence. For at least half an hour, he worked carefully.

At last, he stopped and sucked in his breath.

"Look!" His voice was husky and taut. There, beneath the mineral light was a small, glowing object.

"Is that it?" Felicia asked, reaching out to pick it up.

The object moved, and she screamed involuntarily.

"You'd better be careful about what you pick up around here," he told her. "That's a scorpion."

"A scorpion?" she echoed, shuddering. "Do they fluoresce?"

"Just like the ore-bearing rocks."

A moment later Ed cried out again, triumphantly.

"This time, we've found it!" he shouted. "We've found it!"

CHAPTER 13

STAKING THE CLAIM

Felicia felt her heart pressing against her ribs, and her breath was coming in short, quick gasps.

"Are you sure, Dad?" Sue demanded. It was all she could do to speak.

"Look for yourself, Kitten!" Ed exclaimed.

"I can't believe it," she said numbly. "It isn't true. It can't be!"

Her dad laughed exultantly.

"It's true, all right, and we've beaten Pietro and Spanner. Won't they be surprised when they get here and find that we've already staked it out!"

Joan Bailey glanced around in the darkness, apprehensively. "Just so they don't come and surprise us," she said.

"What are we going to do, Dad?" Sue asked. "You've got to get the claim staked off and file on it, don't you?"

"That's right," he said. He turned to Nina. "The mission has a light plane. We'll mark off the claim, get over to the station, and, as soon as it is light enough to see, I'll have them fly me to Alamos to record the claim."

They all worked with frantic haste to get the claim marked out legally. The perspiration stood out on their faces and soaked their clothes. It seemed to Felicia that they would never finish. Exhaustion stole her strength until her entire being trembled.

"Now," Ed said when the last pillar of rocks was firmly in place, "to get to the mission and see if they will fly me to Alamos."

"Oh, I know they will," Nina said, "after everything you've done for me!"

"It would sure be a bigger favor for me than we did for you, Nina," Ed told her as they mounted once more. "Actually, I suppose it will mean the difference between whether we get our claim or lose it to Pietro and his friends."

"Speaking of them," Joan put in. Her voice betrayed her nervousness. "What if they come along and knock down all those rocks you piled up?"

"There's a big penalty for interfering with claim markers," Ed told her. "I used two natural marks, a big boulder and a crooked tree at a bend in the creek. They can't move them. No, if I get down to Alamos and register the claim first, there's nothing they can do to take it away from us."

He rode on in silence for several minutes.

"I've just been thinking," he said at last. "If this claim does prove out, I'm going to give each of you an interest in it."

"Ed!" Felicia exclaimed in protest. "You shouldn't do that. It isn't fair. All we did is come along and get in your way. It doesn't belong to us."

"We've all been in this thing together," he replied firmly. "If it is valuable, we all ought to share in it."

"Thank you very kindly," Joan said cheerfully. "Just think, when I came out here, I was only scared. Now I'm both scared and rich."

They all laughed.

"You'd better not buy any fancy clothes or diamonds just yet," Ed told her. "You can't spend ore that's still in the ground."

"I can dream, can't I?"

"What would you do with your share," Sue asked Joan, "if it comes through?"

"I don't know," Joan retorted. "I think I'd change it all into pennies and try to get a pile as tall as the Empire State building."

"A very worthy ambition," Ed told her.

"Seriously," Sue repeated.

Joan thought for a moment. "First of all, I'd find some good, worthy Christian work in which to invest my tithe," she said. "Then, I think I'd put the rest of it away in a good, safe place."

"Wouldn't you spend any of it?" Ed asked her curiously.

"At Wellington," Joan said, mimicking the stern voice of the Dean of Women, "girls are taught that there are more valuable things than money. There are good manners, good breeding and culture, and the ability to enjoy oneself and be happy and content regardless of circumstances or environment."

"That's good philosophy," Nina said, "if she only included Jesus Christ."

"You girls are always talking religion. Don't you ever get tired of it?" Ed asked. He spoke pleasantly enough, but there was a trace of irritation in his voice.

"I used to think that too, Dad," Sue said, "but I changed my mind when I realized what Jesus Christ can mean in a person's life."

Ed Collins turned to her curiously. "Now what sort of talk is that?" he asked.

"I'm a Christian now," she explained simply.

"Sue!" he retorted. "I'm surprised to hear you talk that way. You've always been a Christian."

"But I haven't, Dad," she told him. She went on to give her testimony. When she finished, he rode on silently.

"You make a person think, Kitten," he said. "I've always laughed at that sort of talk before. I figured that if a person were kind and moral, he was living well enough to get by."

"That's exactly what I thought," she continued,

"but the Bible says differently. What are those verses, Felicia?"

"Oh, no!" he answered quickly. "I've had enough preaching for tonight."

"But, Dad," Sue said earnestly, "it's not preaching when someone tells you about Jesus Christ and what He can do for you. It's the most important thing in the world."

Ed Collins clucked to his horse.

"I'll tell you one thing, Kitten," he said, "if there's anyone who can get me to thinking that way, it's you."

"Oh, Dad!" Sue exclaimed. "I'd be the happiest girl in the world if you and Tim knew Jesus too."

Ed Collins had been chattering excitedly as they rode, but now he fell silent. He did not speak until at last they saw the lights of the mission.

The superintendent got up in answer to their knock. Hurriedly, Ed told him everything that had happened.

"Sure," he said. "I'll wake the pilot. He'll take you to Alamos just as soon as it's light enough to take off. Our little field isn't lighted, you know."

"That will be great," Ed replied. "Now I think you girls had better go off to bed. You're almost asleep on your feet."

"My wife will show them to their rooms," the superintendent said.

While he was getting his wife, Ed turned to the girls. "I'll take in this ore sample and leave it with the assayer," he said. "If he doesn't have time to do the work on it before we come back so he can tell us what we've got, he can have word for us when we get back to town."

The superintendent came back just in time to hear Ed. "We have a two-way radio now," he said. "It's only been installed a short while, but we can get in touch with them, or they can get in touch with us if they have access to a radio."

"I've got a friend who's a 'ham' operator," Ed said. "I can have him get the information for us and relay it to you."

Ed went to bed but was up an hour before dawn, and as soon as the first, faint gray streaks of morning began to chase the night away, he and the mission pilot went out to the little plane.

Felicia heard them as they took off. She stirred as the sound wakened her slightly, rolled over, and went to sleep again. She and Joan were still in bed at noon when Sue knocked on their door.

Felicia got up as soon as she realized what time it was.

"Why didn't you call me?" she asked. "We shouldn't have slept this long."

"I could have slept another twenty-four hours, I think," Joan said, rubbing her eyes sleepily.

Sue entered the room quietly and sat down.

"Tim got in a little while ago," she said.

"He did?" Joan echoed. "How did he get here so quickly?"

"He met a cow hand who gave him a ride for almost fifteen miles," Sue continued. "He got horses and headed right back. And when he found our note, he came directly here."

"Poor guy!" Felicia said. "I'll bet he's worn out."

"He took a shower and went to bed."

Sue folded her hands in the center of her lap.

"Where do you suppose your dad is by now?" Joan asked. "Do you suppose he beat Spanner to record the claim?"

"It doesn't matter," Sue answered quietly.

"Why?" Felicia demanded. "What do you mean?"

"We got the radio report a little while ago," she said. "It must have come shortly after Dad and the pilot left to come back here, for they haven't arrived yet."

"What did the assayer say about the ore?" Joan asked.

"It isn't scheelite," Sue replied. "There was a trace of scheelite in the samples Dad took but nothing compared to the ore that Pietro found there."

"But I don't see how that could be," Felicia said.

"Perhaps the scheelite-bearing rock was washed there from somewhere upstream," Sue said, "or maybe it was the only piece that had a high concentration of scheelite in it."

"Are they sure?" Joan asked incredulously.

"Positive. The bulk of the fluorescing came from thorium. And it's not worth much."

"Oh, that's too bad!"

It was a long while before Sue spoke.

"Maybe," she said at last, "and maybe not." She picked up the Bible and held it lovingly. "Getting a big lot of money might be the worst thing for Dad and Tim and me. It might make me turn away from God, and it might make Tim and Dad harder to reach with the gospel. And that is the most important thing in the world."

"That's certainly right," Felicia said.

"Besides," Sue continued, "that scheelite-bearing rock came from upstream undoubtedly. Perhaps Dad and Tim will stumble on to the place sometime later, after they have confessed their sin and trusted Christ as their Savior."

"I had never thought of it that way before," Joan said. Her voice was husky.

"As you go back home," Sue began, "will you pray for them?"

"Of course, we will," they both assured her.

"And pray that my life will be a real testimony, that they will see Christ in me and be drawn to Him."

Felicia looked at her. And in that moment, she realized that Sue was completely serious about the mine. There was no regret, no disappointment in her eyes. Only concern for Tim and their dad, that they, too, would become Christians.

"We'll be praying for you, Sue," Felicia said softly.

THE
FELICIA CARTRIGHT SERIES

Felicia Cartright, a petite blonde who is one of the most popular students at Wellington School for Girls, has a surprising inclination toward mysteries. If a mysterious situation arises, it either makes its way to Felicia, or Felicia somehow finds it. Though this is a bit trying for her happy-go-lucky roommate, Joan Bailey, it does prevent life from becoming monotonous. It also enables Bernard Palmer, the popular author of the "Danny Orlis" books, to write an entertaining series of stories for girls aged twelve to eighteen.

The mysteries range from a valuable missing antique to an attempt by claim jumpers to steal a deposit of tungsten ore. There's excitement and action galore—but there's also spiritual guidance and blessing because Felicia and her partner-in-adventure love the Lord and take Him into account in all their experiences.

AVAILABLE FROM WWW.ANEKOPRESS.COM